MENSA

PUBLICATIONS

MIGHTY

BRAIN TEASERS

MENSA
PUBLICATIONS

MIGHTY
BRAIN TEASERS

Robert Allen
Josephine Fulton

CARLTON

THIS IS A CARLTON BOOK

Text copyright © Mensa Limited 1995
Design and artwork copyright © Carlton Books Limited 1995

This edition published by Carlton Books Limited 1995

A CIP catalogue for this book is available from the British Library

ISBN 1-85868-141-3

Printed in Great Britain

C O N T E N T S

Mensa thrives on the notion that mental activity is fun. Whether that activity involves unraveling the secrets of a cunningly constructed puzzle or investigating the complex workings of the human mind makes no difference – the fascination lies in testing our mental faculties to their fullest extent.

This book gives you the opportunity to stretch your mental powers in numerous ways. The *Riddles & Conundrums* section was devised as a series of puzzles of widely differing types that would give many hours of mind-taxing amusement. We have included lateral-thinking problems, matchstick puzzles, word games, numerical problems, and many more. In all there are over 200 opportunities to test your mental agility. In terms of value for money this is not a book that will simply occupy you on a train journey (unless your train happens to be the Trans-Siberian Railway).

If you want to try a different sort of challenge we have compiled a battery of tests designed to increase your knowledge of your personality and abilities. The tests are designed to be fun and will help you to decide in what direction your talents may lie. Do you have good concentration? Are you better with words than with numbers? Do you have good aesthetic judgment? All these questions are tackled in the second section,

Know Yourself. Freud urged his followers to begin psychoanalysis by working on themselves. After all, who knows you better? Psychometric tests are expensive to create and are only used by trained psychologists. However, the tests in this book can give you some interesting isights into your mental processes. But remember, if you want to make important decisions based on psychometric testing do get qualified professional advice first. Mensa does provide a psychometric testing service and you can contact us at: Mensa Psychometrics, Mensa House, St John's Square, Wolverhampton WV2 4AH, England. American Mensa Limited is at 2626 E 14th Street, Brooklyn, New York 11235-3992.

Robert Allen,
Editorial Director, Mensa Publications (UK).

In the time it takes you to crack a handful of the Supersleuth lateral thinking puzzles contained within this book, you could have mowed the lawn, washed the car, or wallpapered the guest bedroom. The fiendishly cunning puzzles in this section will occupy hours that you could have devoted to higher and nobler causes, or you could have paid a surprise visit to friends. But there is nothing more enjoyable or more satisfying than solving puzzles, and here are puzzles of every kind in abundance.

If you like puzzles you will like Mensa. It is probably the only society in the world that you get to join just by being good at puzzling. We have over 120,000 members throughout the world so, wherever you live, there is probably a branch near you. An address to contact Mensa is given in the Foreword, on pages 6-7. Robert Allen and Josephine Fulton would like to thank Tim Sell for his excellent illustrations in this section of *MIGHTY BRAIN TEASERS*.

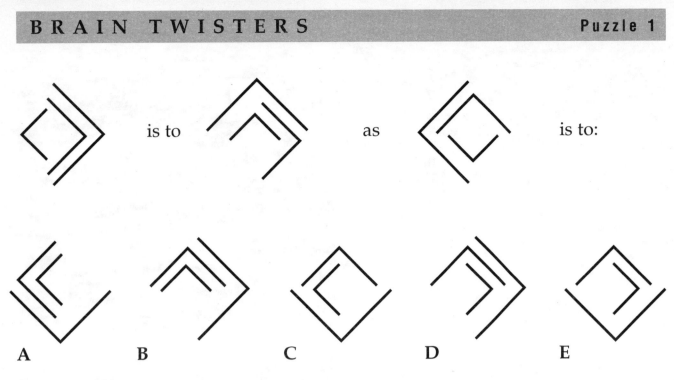

is to ... as ... is to:

A   B   C   D   E

See answer 190.

Which is the odd one out?

A   B   C

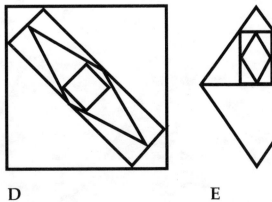

See answer 42.   D   E

'I know a question which can never be answered "Yes",' said Sam. 'So do I,' said Joe. 'How about "Are you a gorilla?", I could never answer that with a yes.' 'Oh, yes you could,' objected Sam. 'You would just have to lie. The question I have in mind could never be answered with a yes even by the most brazen liar.' What was the question Sam had in mind?

See answer 64.

Which of the following forms a perfect triangle when combined with the picture on the right?

A   B

See answer 191.

C   D   E

1 Insert the correct mathematical signs to make the following calculations work:

7 8   20   32 = 44   6 7   15   13 = 44

9 3   42   12 = 94.5   5 32   6   20 = 18.75

8 2   12   9 = 37   *See answer 151.*

2 Look at the clock faces shown below. Choose one to continue the series.

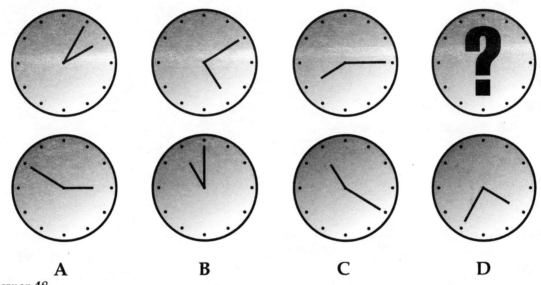

A   B   C   D

See answer 48.

Which is the odd one out?

A   B   C   D   E

See answer 181.

1 A frog sits on a lily pad in the precise middle of a circular pond with a radius of 6 metres (19 feet). He jumps straight towards the edge of the pond a distance of 3 metres (9 ft, 6 ins) but this tires him and every subsequent jumps is precisely half the distance of the jump before (ie, 1.5 metres (4 ft 9 ins), 75cm (2 ft, 4 ins), etc). How many jumps does it take him to reach the edge of the pond?

See answer 6.

2 How many grooves were there on an old-fashioned vinyl record?

See answer 49.

3 Which is correct, 'All fish have warm blood' or 'All fishes are warm-blooded'?

See answer 54.

4 Alex and Georgina were born at the same hour of the same day to the same mother in the same hospital. They have the same father and yet they are not twins. Why ?

See answer 118.

By taking away four matches from this diagram leave eight small squares.

See answer 144.

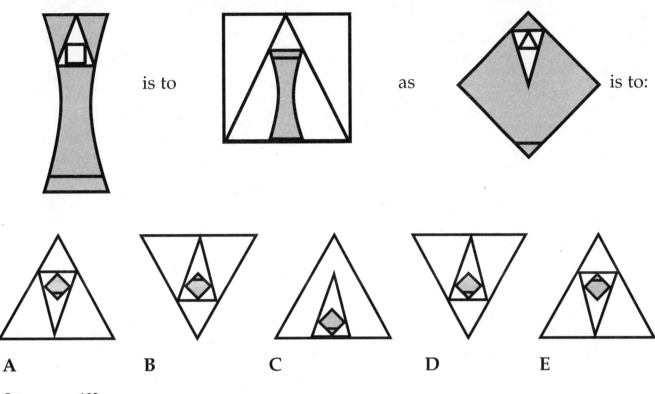

A   **B**   **C**   **D**   **E**

See answer 192.

The British used to use gold sovereigns. The 1883 sovereign contained exactly the same amount of gold as the 1884 one. Even so, 1884 sovereigns are worth more than 1883 sovereigns. Why? There is no special historical significance to the date 1883.

See answer 63.

Which is the odd one out?

A   B   C   D   E

See answer 193.

After a VIP party, the floor was littered with the torn up name tags of the rich and famous. Try to put them back together to discover the guest list. All the guests were actors.

MO RO THAU MAT ORE WAL

MAR ROB JO MAN LEW

TER LON LEN ALE DAY SKI

FORD BRAN IEL RED CY

CAR AL IS DIA DY

AN BILL ERT SHEP TER

FOS DIN HERD DUD DO

CLAU DAN WOO DIE LEY POL

See answer 168.

1 Before Sir Richard Burton attempted to discover the source of the Nile what was the world's longest river?

See answer 1.

2 Though the discoverers of Antarctica (South Pole) were often close to starvation they would never touch the meat of the Polar Bear even though they possessed the means to kill one. Why?

See answer 17.

3 The shamans of Central Asia knew of an ancient and ingenious means of passing right through solid walls. What was it?

See answer 30.

4 In the early 18th century Mrs Abigail Eischrank of Cambridge, Massachusetts, gave birth to 13 children. Exactly half of them were girls. Explain.

See answer 46.

5 Leonardo da Vinci carried out the following experiment. He held a sphere of very thin fragile glass above a floor of solid stone. When he dropped it the sphere fell two metres (6 feet, 6 inches) without breaking. How?

See answer 5.

Another series of clock faces. Again it is up to you to work out the logic behind the series and pick a clock to replace the question mark.

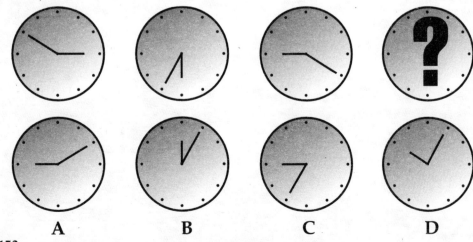

A   B   C   D

See answer 153.

1 The diagram above is made up of matchsticks and represents a dry martini with an olive in the glass. Move one matchstick to place the olive outside the glass.

See answer 60.

2 This is a very old American puzzle but it has lost none of its tantalizing qualities with the passage of time. The diagram represents a round tablecloth. You have a supply of eggs and are invited to place one on the cloth. Your opponent then takes a turn. No eggs must be touching and you are not allowed to move an egg once it has been placed. The winner is the person who places the last egg. There is a way to win every time. What is it?

See answer 7.

QUICK WIT   Puzzle 16

*I*n 1993, 78-year-old Sergeant Noboru Yamamoto was discovered living on a remote Pacific island firmly under the impression that World War II was still on. He was eventually persuaded to return to Japan, where he was immediately surrounded by his remaining relatives and hordes of journalists. Suddenly a young man pushed to the front of the crowd, shot Yamamoto several times, and then swiftly left the room. No one took the slightest notice. Why? The young man did not know the sergeant and his motive was not any form of revenge.

See answer 9.

1 What has 21 spots but is never ill?

See answer 80.

2 What was the first man-made object to travel faster than the speed of sound?
See answer 62.

Which is the odd one out?

b   T   W   o   u

A   B   C   D   E

See answer 22.

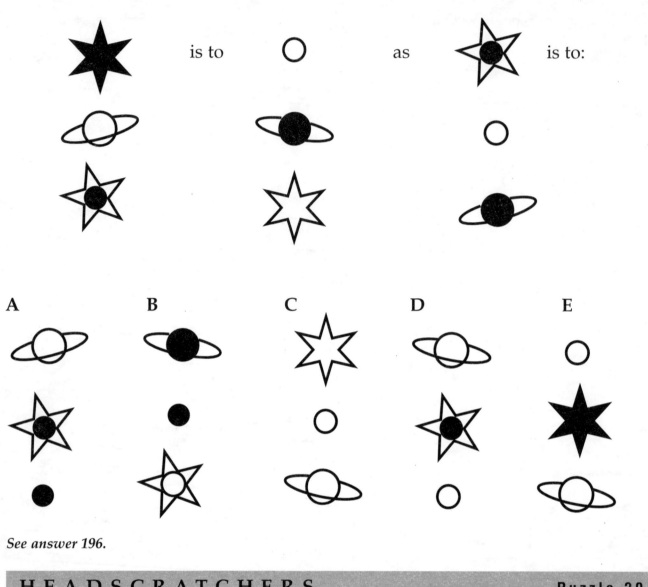

See answer 196.

Which is the odd one out?

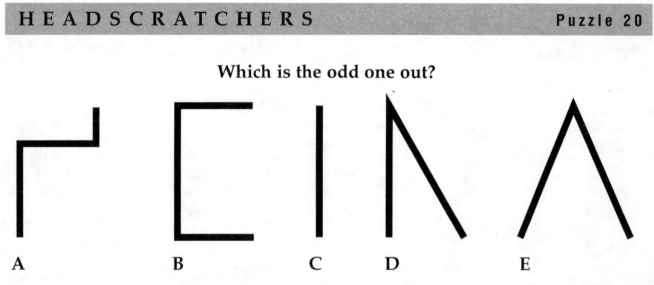

See answer 213.

is to   as   is to:

A   B   C   D   E

See answer 182.

Someone has made a mistake decorating this
cake. Can you correct the pattern?

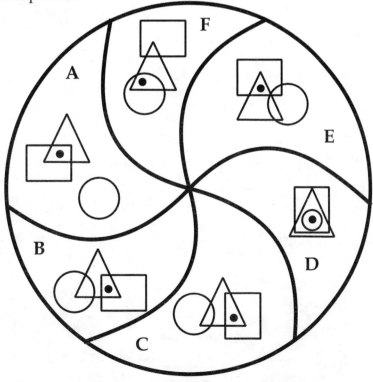

See answer 156.

1 Dave went with his uncle to the movies. They went up to the ticket kiosk and Dave had to pay, as usual. But that was not the worst of it. The ticket lady said, 'You can go in but not your friend.' Why wouldn't she let Dave's uncle in? He was smartly dressed and had often been to that cinema before without any trouble.

See answer 31.

2 In a run-down saloon in a small town west of the Pecos, One-Eyed Pete and his gang sat playing poker. There were five men round the table. A rougher, tougher looking bunch you never saw in your life. Just to be allowed to join the gang you had to skin your own grandma with a rusty potato peeler. After several games one of the men eyed the dealer narrowly and drawled, 'I says you're cheatin'!' It was an unwise comment. The dealer whipped out a gun and shot the offender dead. Naturally someone sent for the sheriff. He was a giant of a man who never went anywhere without two Colt .45s hanging from his belt. He was so mean and tough that he had skinned both his grandmas in a manner too horrible to relate. However, even though he was a stranger to fear, and the incident had been witnessed by everyone in the bar, he was unable to arrest any of the men who had taken part in the game. Why?

See answer 82.

Which of the following comes next in the sequence? *See answer 184.*

A   B   C   D   E

In the pioneer days of America a man lived on his ranch a few miles out of town. One night his wife was taken sick and he had to ride into town to get a doctor. He owned three horses but one was itself sick, another was too old to make the trip and there was no way he was ever going to ride the third. Why not?

He had only just bought the third horse and there was nothing wrong with it or with himself. In the stable there was no shortage of saddles and tack. What was the problem?

See answer 26.

HEADSCRATCHERS

The circles of letters below contain the names of three works of literature (one French, one from the Middle East, one American). Can you unravel them?

See answer 160.

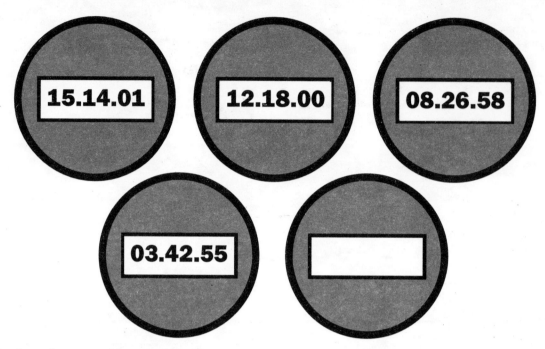

Have a look at these strange watches. By cracking the logic which connects them you should be able to work out what time should be shown on the face of the fifth watch.

See answer 66.

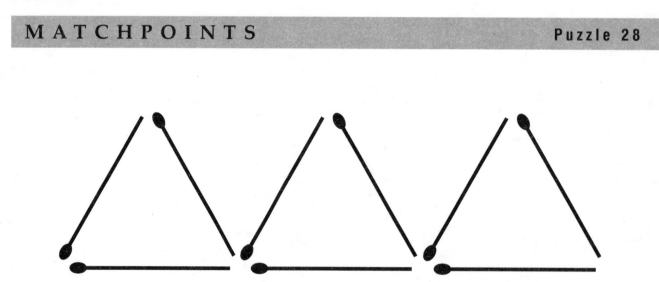

Take 9 matches and lay them out in three triangles. By moving three matches try to make five triangles.

See answer 141.

If you look at the grid carefully you will be able to find the names of three international airports cunningly concealed. The names wind through the grid like a snake so, once you have discovered one of them, it should be possible to discover the others.

See answer 157.

1 Sue Sugar had toothache. She went to the only dentists in town where she was greeted by Dr Molar and Dr Bicuspid, the partners. She noticed that whereas Dr Molar had a wonderful mouthful of teeth, his partner's teeth seemed in urgent need of attention. With which partner should she book her appointment?

See answer 33.

2 Six men drove over 240 km (150 miles) in a car at an average speed of 100 k/h (62.5 mph). The trip took 2.4 hours. When they unpacked their luggage they realised that the car had a flat during the whole journey. Why had they not noticed this before?

See answer 27.

Which of the following forms a perfect circle when combined with the diagram on the right?

See answer 183.

A   B

C   D   E

1 A train crossing from France to Germany suffered a terrible accident exactly on the border. According to international law in which country should the survivors be buried?

See answer 198.

2 Are there earthquakes on the Moon?

See answer 23.

Use 16 matches to make this figure. Now add eight more matches to divide the shape into four equal pieces.

See answer 149.

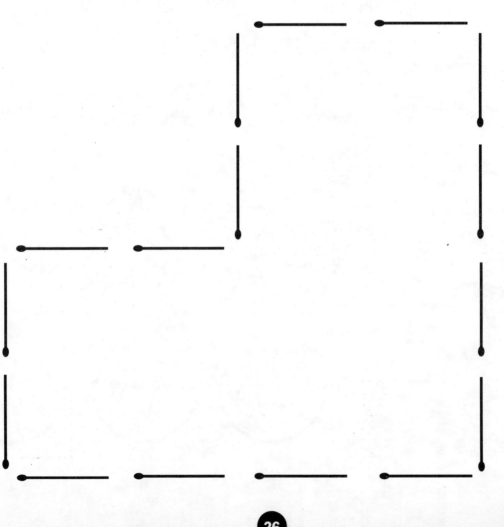

What comes next in the sequence?

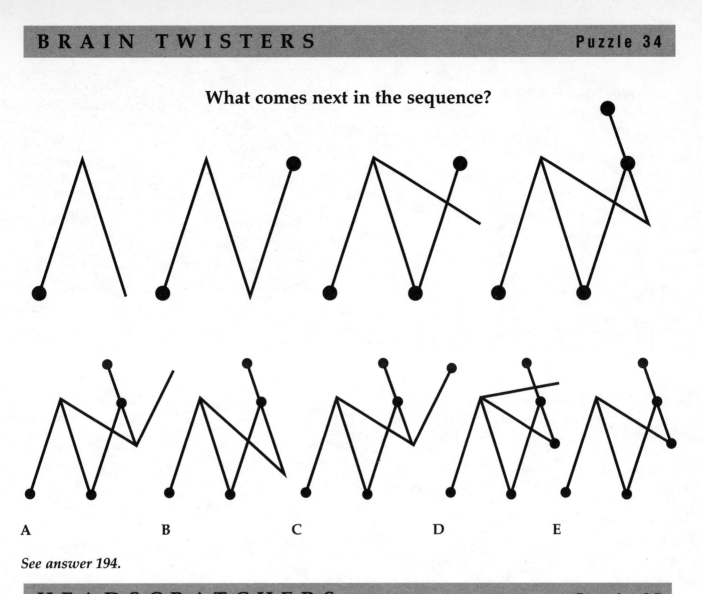

A   B   C   D   E

See answer 194.

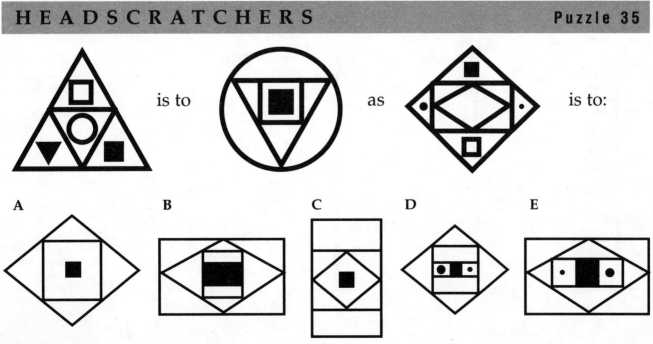

is to ... as ... is to:

A   B   C   D   E

See answer 215.

Which cube can be made using:

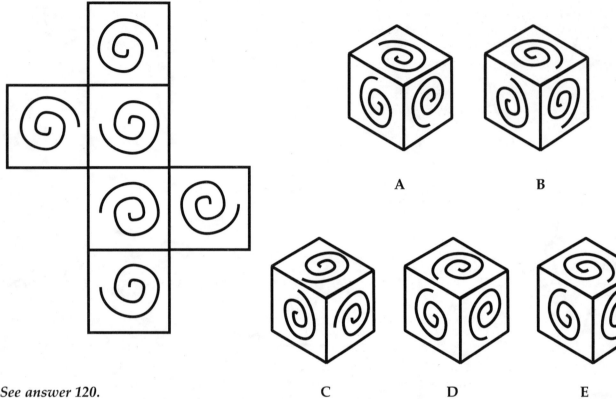

A

B

C

D

E

See answer 120.

Which is the odd one out?

A   B   C   D   E

See answer 78.

Ali ben-Ibrahim was a salt dealer in old Baghdad. Every day he went from his home just outside the city to the market with two huge sacks of salt tied to the back of his donkey. His donkey was a small, evil-smelling brute called Roxanna. It was, however, not lacking in the brains department. One hot day, as they passed along the banks of the Tigris, it broke free from Ali and plunged into the cool water. When the irate salt-seller finally persuaded the beast to leave the river it immediately noticed that much of the salt had dissolved and its load was therefore considerably lighter. After that, no matter how hard Ali tried, he could not prevent the donkey from diving into the river and ruining its load of salt. But when it came to lateral thinking Ali himself was no slouch. One day he loaded up the donkey as usual and, as usual, the animal plunged into the river. Then it learned its lesson and never tried that trick again. What had Ali done?

See answer 34.

1 When the police arrived the man was lying under the car dead. Investigations revealed that although he was not the car's owner he was the last person to drive it. The car had last been driven that morning but the man's time of death was established at about 3pm. The car's owner was discovered in the south of France. No one else was involved in the affair and eventually the police and the coroner were satisfied that no crime had been committed. What is the explanation?

See answer 28.

2 Andy's aunt had lived all her adult life in Los Angeles having moved there when she married an American. She had lost touch with Andy's mother, her sister, for over 25 years. Then she suddenly wrote to say she was coming back for a holiday. Andy's mother gave him the flight number and asked him to pick his aunt up from Heathrow Airport. 'But how will I recognize her, I've never even seen a photograph!' he objected. 'And she's never seen a photograph of you,' added his mother cheerfully. 'But don't worry you won't miss her.' And he didn't, but how?

See answer 195.

What comes next in the sequence?

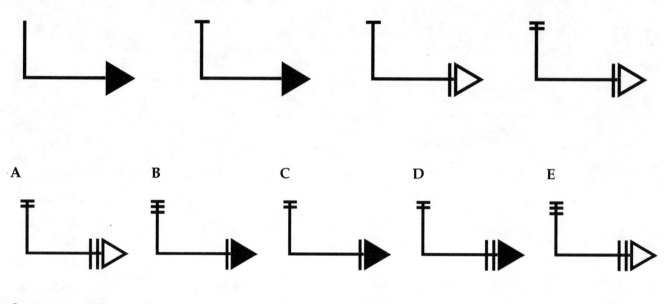

A   B   C   D   E

See answer 119.

Which of the following will be shaped like the diagram below if a single line of any shape but not overlapping any existing line, is added?

A   B

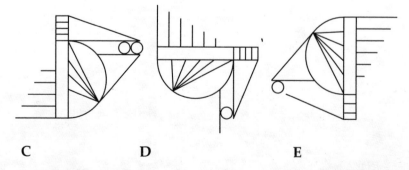

C   D   E

See answer 200.

Professor Potts has had a disaster. A shelf in his museum gave way and ten priceless busts of Roman emperors have been smashed. Fortunately, each had a name plate on it. Can you put the fractured names back together?

AU PA TI VALE
NE TIAN
DIO AU GAL CA BER DI
TUS LA US TRA GUS SIAN
RO BA VES CL CLE
IUS RIAN LI GU JAN

See answer 170.

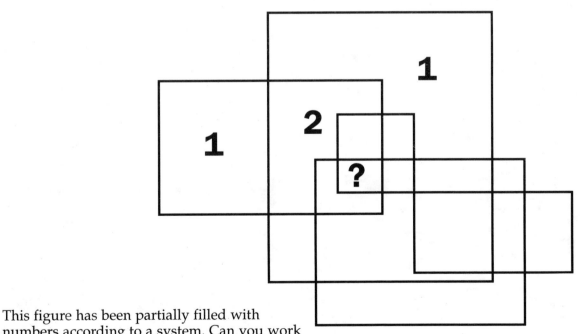

This figure has been partially filled with numbers according to a system. Can you work out the logic of the system and replace the question mark with a number?

See answer 68.

Try to work out the fiendish logic behind this series of clocks and replace the question mark.

See answer 154.

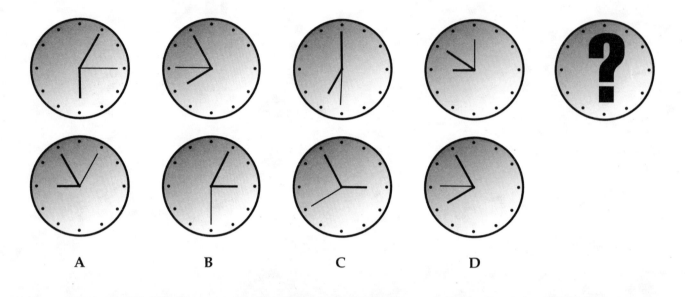

A   B   C   D

Which is the odd one out?

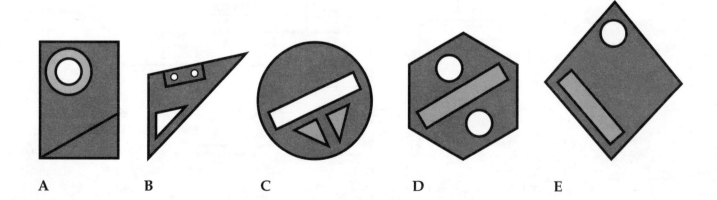

A   B   C   D   E

See answer 185.

1 After a long and arduous journey your ship reaches the sea which is your destination. However, there is no water to be seen anywhere. In fact there never was any water and you knew that perfectly well before you set out. So why did you navigate your ship to this sea?

See answer 163.

2 Sid Lightly always moans that if only people told the truth he would sell more of his goods. What does he make?

See answer 18.

3 Thomas and Craig go collecting sea shells. They take bag with them to hold their booty. Without knowing its dimensions can you work out how many sea shells they can put in the empty bag?

See answer 199.

4 Albert Coley is a fishmonger. He stands 6ft 6ins (2 metres) in his socks, takes size XXL in clothes and wears size 14 (50) shoes. What do you think he weighs?

See answer 127.

5 Sam Somnolent wanted a good night's rest. He went to bed at 8.30pm, wound up his 30-year-old alarm clock and set it to wake him at 9am. How many hours' sleep did Sam get?

See answer 211.

6 A man and his wife were driving rapidly through town late at night. Suddenly the car broke down. The man had to get help but was nervous about leaving his wife alone at that hour. However, there was absolutely no question of her coming too. Eventually he told her to lock all the doors, keep the windows shut and wait for him to return. Under no circumstances whatsoever was she to let anyone else into the car. The wife did as she was told, but, even so, when the man returned to the locked car his wife was entertaining two strangers. What had happened?

See answer 15.

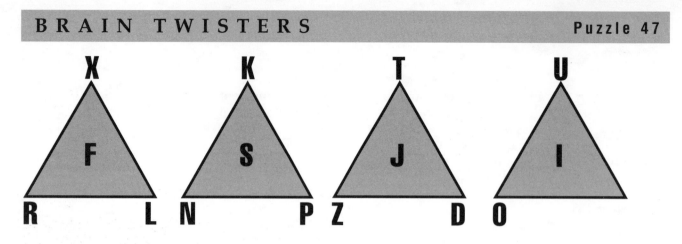

Look at these triangles. Can you work out what the missing letter is? *See answer 88.*

SUPER SLEUTH   Puzzle 48

1 How many times can you divide 345.6754 by 23.854?

See answer 36.

2 Ben Bright was a smart kid. He bet all the other kids in his class that they couldn't stick a pin in a fully inflated balloon without bursting it. He was right, they couldn't. Each loser had to give him their lunch money and by the end of the day he was quite rich. The other kids insisted that the trick was impossible but Ben did it easily. How?

See answer 19.

3 Young Ben Bright had another good idea. He bet his friends that they couldn't take hold of the ends of a piece of string and, without letting go, tie a knot in the middle of the string. After they had all failed miserably he showed them how it was done. What did he do?

See answer 164.

QUICK WIT   Puzzle 49

Khalil ben-Omar became Calif of Baghdad. Shortly after taking up his new position one of his advisors pointed out to him a little scruffy fellow riding a donkey in through the city gates. 'That man,' said the advisor, 'is a trader from Pakistan. His name is Zulfiqa Khan and he is the biggest rogue in the entire country. Don't let his appearance fool you. He's hugely rich and for years he has been making a fortune out of smuggling but we've never been able to catch him at it.' The Calif was intrigued and ordered that the smuggler should be searched rigorously every he time he entered or left the city. So each day Zulfiqa came riding into the city on his donkey and each day he was searched. Each evening he left on his donkey and each evening he was searched. Nothing was found. But all the time he grew richer and richer. At last the Calif could stand it no longer and he had Zulfiqa summoned to him. 'All right,' he said. 'I admit defeat'. You have been smuggling for years and I have never caught you. Just tell me how you did it and I will let you marry my daughter and make you one of the richest men in Baghdad.' What was Zulfiqa Khan smuggling?

See answer 116.

1 Sergeant Smashem of the Traffic Division reported an accident. A truck and twelve cars had been crushed when a bridge collapsed on them. The truck was badly damaged but the driver escaped from the cab without injury. When the sergeant arrived on the scene, there was no sign of any car drivers. Why not? There was no suggestion that any car driver was in any way to blame for the accident.

See answer 39.

2 One month of the year, February, has 28 or 29 days. How many months have 30 days?

See answer 10.

3 Sam Midas the Director of Midas Inc phones his wife to say he'll be home for dinner. 'Hi, honey, I'm just leaving the office now and I'll be home in ten minutes.' 'OK, darling,' says his wife, 'I'll see you soon.' Sam lives very near his office so he leaves at 6.30 and arrives home at 6.43. Just as he is getting out of the car his wife rushes from the house, boxes his ears and shouts, 'If you ever do that again I'll divorce you!' What did Sam do?

See answer 206.

4 A woman dropped a few coins in a beggar's bowl. The woman is the beggar's sister but the beggar is not the woman's brother. How are they related?

See answer 197.

All these famous playrights have had the vowels removed from their names and the first name joined to the surname. Can you sort them out? (The nationalities are given in brackets to help you.)

1. DWRDLB (American)
2. SMLBCKTT (Irish)
3. BRTHLTBRCHT (German)
4. NLCWRD (English)
5. NTNCHKV (Russian)

6. RTHRMLLR (American)
7. LGPRNDLL (Italian)
8. JNRCN (French)
9. SPHCLS (Greek – one word)
10. TNNSSWLLMS (American)

See answer 161.

is to as is to:

A   **B**   **C**   **D**   **E**

See answer 201.

Which of the following can be constructed using:

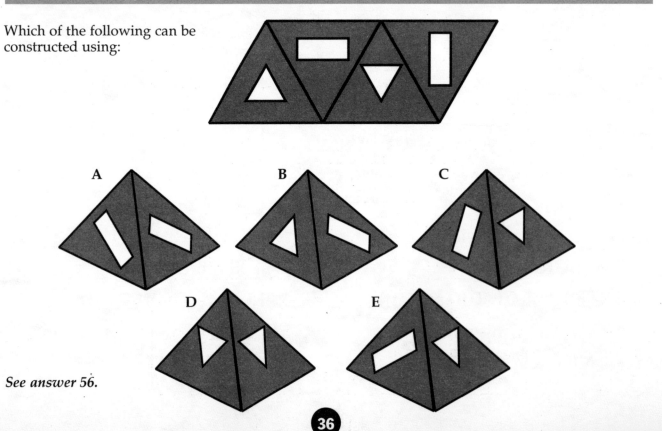

See answer 56.

1 If a man lives in Seattle why can't he be buried in Birmingham?

See answer 2.

2 Do the British have a Fourth of July?

See answer 203.

3 Dave and his brother Bob married Sue and Hannah who are both sisters. However Dave and Bob have different in-laws. How can this be?

See answer 45.

Hidden in this grid are 11 international airports. The names follow each other and meander in a snake-like route through the grid. When you discover the first name you should be able to find the other 10.

See answer 158.

D	A	L	A	M	A	N	D	A	R
E	H	M	A	A	L	A	S	S	E
R	O	N	E	B	I	T	T	E	N
A	C	A	R	K	Z	E	R	A	U
H	H	E	B	E	N	I	T	O	J
O	I	L	L	U	A	G	E	D	S
Y	M	S	O	C	H	A	R	L	E
O	I	A	P	L	E	N	O	T	S
C	N	H	C	I	T	Y	H	O	U
C	M	W	O	R	H	T	A	E	H

Which of the following comes next in the sequence?

Y	V	S	P
H	J	M	Q
P	H	D	B

A	B	C	D	E
M	Q	N	M	Q
V	U	T	V	V
B	A	B	A	B

See answer 202.

Which is the odd one out?

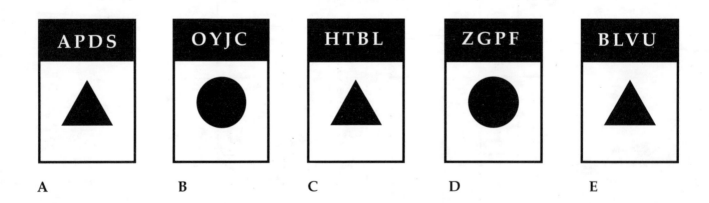

A   B   C   D   E

See answer 44.

Which is the odd one out?

See answer 188.

A friend of mine used to bet unwary tourists a pint of beer that they couldn't take six matches and lay them out in such a way that each touched the other five. He was never known to pay for his own beer!

See answer 150.

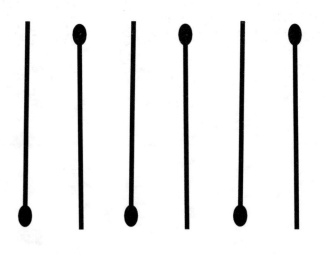

Take a postcard and a pair of scissors. Now cut the postcard in such a way that you can step right through the hole in the middle. Impossible? No, with a little ingenuity you should be able to create a hole through which your entire body can pass.

See answer 77.

Espana

1 Jim White watched in exasperation as the soccer team he had led to world fame over five years was trounced by Brazil. It was just awful! No matter how much he bellowed advice and encouragement nobody took the slightest notice. He almost wept with sheer frustration. At last the whole dismal affair was over and Brazil won by such a huge margin that it went into the record books. Yet, oddly, when the next day's newspapers came out, Jim, far from being attacked, was extravagantly praised. Why?

See answer 51.

2 A man went to the garage to have an electrical fault on his car repaired. Unfortunately the mechanic was ill and therefore the work could not be done. Determined not to waste his trip the man decided to put his car through the car wash. He closed the sun roof, retracted the radio aerial, drove the car into the tunnel and then got out and waited outside for the washing to begin. It was only when he had pushed the button and the washing cycle had started that the man began to bellow with rage. Why?

See answer 16.

The Wigan Philharmonia Orchestra was touring America for the first time and things were not going well. Their performances had been widely criticized and, in particular Albert Winterbottom, the conductor, had come in for some sharp criticism. One evening after a particularly awful peformance a man in the audience stood up and yelled,'Winterbottom, you shouldn't be allowed out, after what you did to that score you should be a butcher instead of a musician!' Albert, unable to stand any more criticism, pulled a gun and shot the man dead in front of the entire audience. The trial was a foregone conclusion and, before long Albert Winterbottom faced the electric chair. However, no matter how many times they tried to execute him nothing happened. The equipment was dismantled, checked, put together again and still didn't work. Why?

See answer 81.

1 Police Officer Gribble was on patrol when he noticed a small girl turn the corner and pass him going down the street. He smiled as she passed but took no further notice. After a few minutes walk the girl came round the corner again and, once more she passed him. This had happened three more times and each time the girl seemed more agitated. At last he could stand it no longer. 'Why are you walking round and round the block,' he demanded. What was the reply?

See answer 53.

2 Emily was delighted when she found that frogs had settled in the garden pond. Sometimes there was a big green one, sometimes a brown, and she saw a couple of little ones too. Then she got to wondering just how many frogs actually lived in the pond. She tried to count them but could never reach the same total twice. Once she was quite sure there were six when, without warning, a completely new frog appeared. Without draining the pond what would be the best way of finding how many frogs there are?

See answer 4.

The pictures illustrate different views of one cube. What does the side indicated by the X look like?

A   B   C   D   E

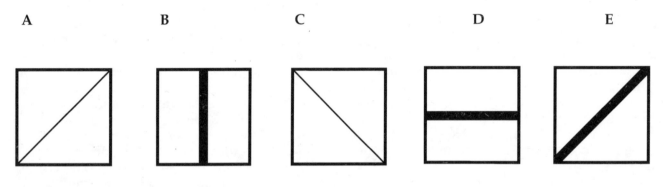

See answer 13.

Which of the following patterns will match the conditions of the diagram below if a single straight line is added?

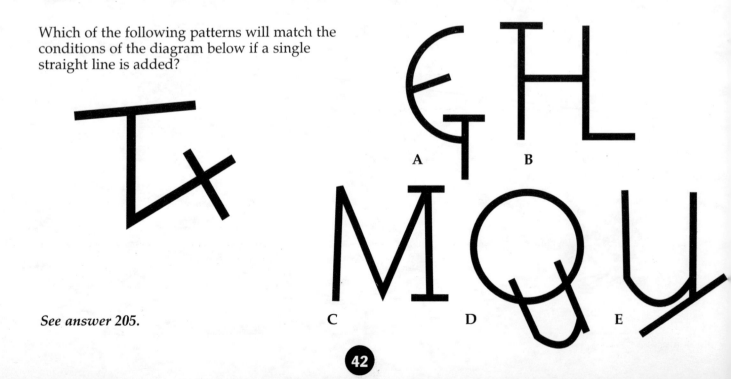

See answer 205.

1 In Dead Men's Gulch, Colorado, there was a barber who had a hold over the local mayor. The mayor was manipulated into passing a law that no man might shave himself and no man might grow a beard. This was all very well and the barber did well out of it but, nevertheless, even one so rich was not above the law. Who shaved the barber?

See answer 65.

2 Victor Serebriakoff, International President of Mensa, once made up a poem about hyperbolic acid, a substance so corrosive that it would eat its way through anything. One day Sir Clive Sinclair, the inventor and British Mensa Chairman, phoned his old friend with some stunning news: 'Victor, you'll never believe this but I have actually invented your hyperbolic acid! Stay where you are and I'll dash round to your house with a flask of it right now.' Victor replaced the phone and chuckled to himself. How could he tell he was being teased?

See answer 11.

Which of the following comes next in the sequence?

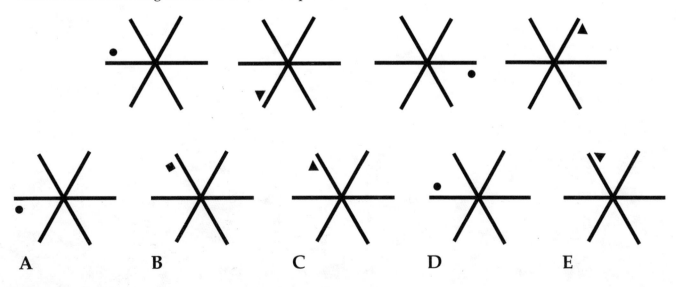

A   B   C   D   E

See answer 187.

You are lost in Paris, but if you search carefully you will find the following well-known places cunningly concealed. Names may be spelt in any direction, not necessarily in a straight line.

RUE DE RIVOLI   BOIS DE BOULOGNE
MOULIN ROUGE   CHAMPS ELYSEES
CLICHY   RUE LAFAYETTE
PERE LACHAISE   SACRE COEUR
ARC DE TRIOMPHE

MADELEINE   MONTMARTRE
OPERA   GARE DE LYON
LOUVRE   JARDIN DES PLANTES

See answer 165.

M	I	F	T	E	P	Z	L	E	I	R	U	E	P	D	T	M	E	R	B
A	A	D	I	H	U	Z	N	E	S	H	A	L	E	R	O	H	N	E	O
N	G	D	H	T	E	I	E	M	S	A	A	E	R	M	S	U	E	M	I
C	H	H	E	S	E	Y	O	E	S	F	G	S	E	U	T	B	L	U	S
A	R	D	E	L	L	I	W	N	A	F	A	O	L	E	I	I	L	T	D
G	A	R	D	E	O	N	D	E	I	Y	Y	N	A	W	N	L	L	R	E
Y	T	R	E	O	A	M	T	H	M	R	E	I	C	L	H	R	A	S	B
O	D	E	C	H	D	E	P	E	O	W	T	L	H	T	E	Y	O	S	O
U	T	H	C	T	Y	A	R	S	P	S	T	E	A	F	R	A	N	U	U
M	E	A	T	H	E	C	O	M	E	O	Z	E	D	I	O	D	E	G	L
M	J	A	R	D	I	N	D	O	U	L	E	G	S	S	A	C	R	E	O
C	H	C	T	P	R	E	E	R	N	H	Y	R	E	R	U	E	O	C	G
A	R	A	E	R	S	A	S	A	D	T	I	S	D	J	U	I	K	H	N
T	C	A	R	S	A	D	P	F	N	I	S	E	I	S	T	L	E	T	E
C	T	O	H	C	I	S	L	E	L	I	B	E	R	T	E	L	I	L	E
L	E	P	R	E	D	D	A	N	T	E	S	S	E	A	Y	L	T	T	S
I	Y	E	S	T	E	G	M	T	M	O	N	T	M	A	R	T	R	E	O
C	T	R	E	T	Y	R	U	E	D	E	R	I	V	O	L	I	D	O	N
H	H	A	R	W	A	T	H	E	Y	A	B	E	E	N	E	T	U	O	R
Y	N	D	I	O	M	P	H	E	H	V	E	L	O	U	V	R	E	E	A

Captain Franklin and his crew were lost in the icy sea off Greenland. Food was low and, what was worse, they had run out of water. 'If we drink the sea water we'll die,' said the First Mate. 'No need for that, Mr MacTavish,' replied Franklin, 'the sea water round here is quite drinkable.' What did he mean?

See answer 50.

HEADSCRATCHERS

1 Look in a mirror. You left hand seems to have become your right and your right is now apparently your left. You have been laterally reversed! Why does the mirror not reverse you vertically as well?

See answer 117.

2 What has three hands, the second hand really being the third?

See answer 3.

3 Two men are charged with murder. One committed the act but the other is quite innocent. The judge is in a quandry as to how to punish the guilty whilst letting the innocent man go free. Finally he calls for an eminent doctor to advise him. Why?

See answer 84.

4 Smart Alec sat in biology class with a smug grin on his face. 'What are you looking so pleased about?' asked the teacher with a feeling of impending doom. 'I know something that has four legs and two arms,' announced Alec proudly. The teacher racked his brains but could think of no creature which fitted the description. What did Alec mean?

See answer 71.

5 'You're really going to fly around the Earth from North to South?' said the young man to the aviator. 'I'll bet you'll need your thermal underwear when you pass over the Poles!' 'Actually,' the intrepid flyer replied, 'the Poles are the least of my worries I shall have to pass twice over a much colder area than that.' What could it be?

See answer 125.

1 What is the missing letter in this series:

B C D E I K O X

See answer 83.

2 Which letter can complete this series:

A H I M O U V W X Y

See answer 47.

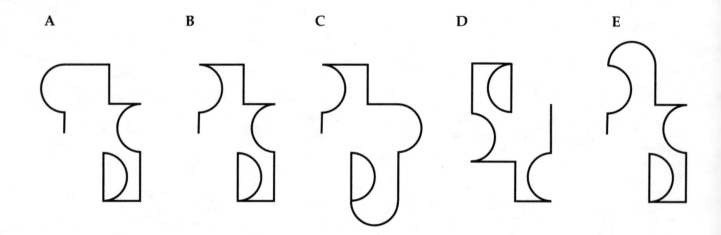

See answer 41.

1 You are walking down the road when suddenly there is a terrific bang. A bomb has exploded. You look round and, to your horror, see a scene of dreadful carnage with bodies lying all over the road. Miraculously, though you are only a few feet away, you are completely unscathed. How could this be?

See answer 55.

2 A man with a phobia about doctors notices a large black growth has appeared on his head. Even though he has no medical or surgical experience he manages successfully to remove the growth. How?

See answer 221.

3 Why do English men use more soap than Irish men (without being noticeably cleaner)?

See answer 102.

4 A saloon gambler produces three cards and challenges the other customers to a little wager. The first card is red on both sides, the second is red on one side and white on the other and the third is white on both sides. Then he places a card on the table with the red side showing and said, 'This can't be the white/white card so the other side must be red or white. That makes it an even money bet. I'll bet $10 against your $10 on the colour of the other side.' What are the true odds of the gambler winning?

See answer 38.

SOLVE THIS   Puzzle 74

Take two small coins and place them on a table so that they touch. You may touch one coin but not move it, and move the other but not touch it. How would you insert a book, lengthways, between them.

See answer 123.

*S*am Slick's *uncle was always bragging about his exploits in the war. One day he told me how, as a young captain in the campaign in Normandy, he led his battalion against a vastly superior enemy force and completely routed them. Naturally the hero was decorated for his efforts. Delighted for once to have caught the old devil out Sam shouted, 'Uncle, that's a whopper!' Sam knew little about the war so how could he tell?*

See answer 12.

How much is the question mark worth?

See answer 94.

The values of the segments are 3 consecutive numbers under 10. The blank is worth 7 and the sum of the segments equals 50. What do the black and speckled segments equal?

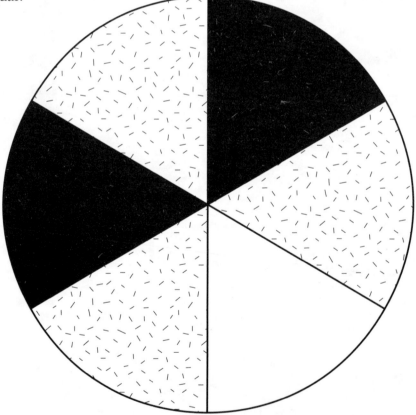

See answer 58.

How much is the question mark worth?

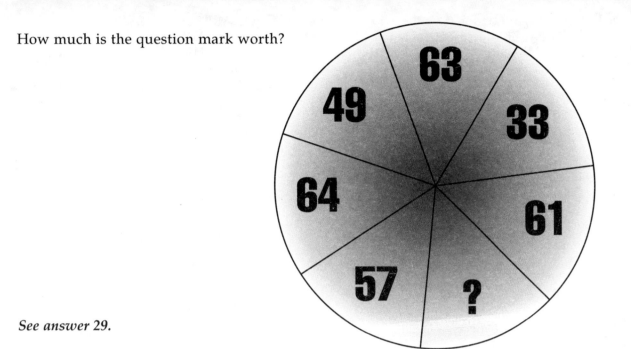

See answer 29.

What letter does the question mark represent ?

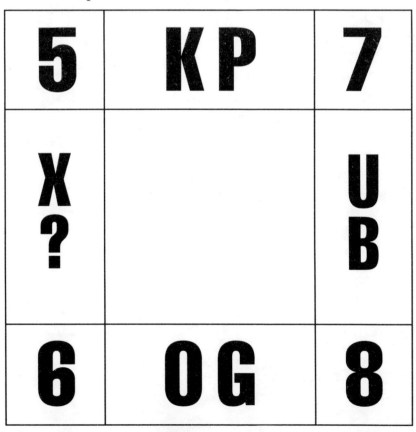

See answer 114.

You have become lost in London. Use the grid to locate the following well-known places. Names may be spelt in any direction, not necessarily in a straight line.

GOLDEN SQUARE
TRAFALGAR SQUARE
PICCADILLY CIRCUS
REGENT'S PARK ZOO
TOWER OF LONDON
BUCKINGHAM PALACE

WESTMINSTER
CHELSEA
KNIGHTSBRIDGE
WATERLOO

CHARING CROSS   WHITEHALL
COVENT GARDEN   HYDE PARK
SOHO   KINGS CROSS

See answer 166.

A	N	O	W	T	H	W	E	S	T	M	I	N	S	T	E	R	E	K	R
B	C	L	A	Q	P	O	D	Y	U	P	D	P	Z	Z	L	E	F	I	I
N	I	H	T	S	I	H	E	S	T	I	Y	U	U	A	R	E	D	N	W
H	A	E	E	C	N	A	R	E	T	L	H	C	E	O	S	E	P	G	E
O	P	R	R	L	C	E	G	O	L	I	N	G	I	T	S	O	C	S	O
U	I	G	L	O	O	A	H	I	U	W	P	S	R	O	M	R	E	C	C
A	S	N	H	T	H	A	D	T	S	H	W	H	C	U	S	A	A	R	T
I	G	C	W	A	S	O	H	O	N	I	T	T	O	K	O	H	G	O	E
R	E	I	R	S	I	M	L	J	G	T	I	N	G	N	W	L	M	S	Y
G	U	T	O	O	T	N	E	D	G	E	H	A	L	L	A	U	N	S	T
A	N	S	D	W	S	S	H	R	T	A	T	D	O	F	B	O	G	K	I
G	O	L	D	E	N	E	T	A	O	F	O	R	A	M	D	Y	N	T	R
O	L	E	B	S	O	U	K	G	W	E	Y	R	U	N	C	K	A	I	L
U	B	A	Q	S	L	R	T	T	E	L	T	F	O	A	P	L	G	H	T
E	I	U	F	Y	A	O	N	U	R	O	F	L	L	A	M	C	A	N	S
R	A	R	O	P	A	E	E	T	H	S	T	A	Y	A	U	E	A	B	Y
E	A	D	E	L	V	R	L	G	I	N	C	S	H	O	R	L	R	L	A
R	A	D	M	O	R	A	L	E	E	E	C	G	P	A	R	I	E	T	Y
E	Y	S	C	A	T	B	U	C	K	I	N	W	H	A	D	Y	N	O	U
H	N	O	T	C	H	E	L	S	E	A	J	O	E	G	R	K	Z	O	O

Mario Peroni, the world famous musician, left his studio window open only to find that the wind had destroyed his precious sheet music. Can you put together the names of 10 famous composers from the pieces shown here?

BARPUCRACH MAN

IUS MAH EL

ZART

RIM

SKY SCHU

SIB

KOR BERTCELL

USMO

OV

CI

DE SAKOV

IN

NI LER

TOK LI

PUR

See answer 35.

Which comes next in the sequence?

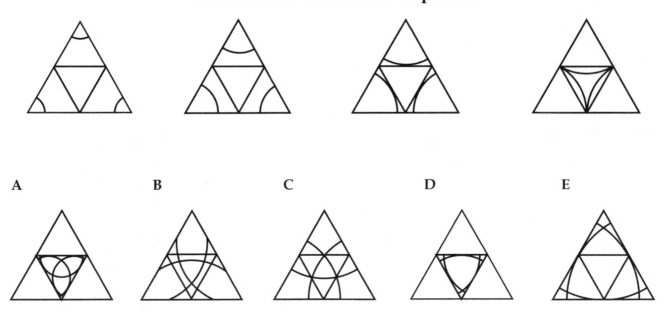

A   B   C   D   E

See answer 207.

1 What can you spend but never buy?

See answer 85.

2 Why are man-hole covers so often round?

See answer 169.

1 A deaf man noticed a bather taking an early morning dip. Just then he saw the tell-tale dorsal fin of a shark approach. In what way could he communicate with the swimmer?

See answer 126.

2 What is the difference between a north wind and a north road?

See answer 37.

1 Use six matches to form four equilateral triangles.

See answer 129.

2 Place three matches on top of three wine glasses in such a way that they will support a pile of coins.

See answer 130.

3 Arrange five matches to add up to fourteen.

See answer 131.

4 Lay down 17 matches so that they form six squares as below. Now remove only five matches and leave just three squares.

See answer 133.

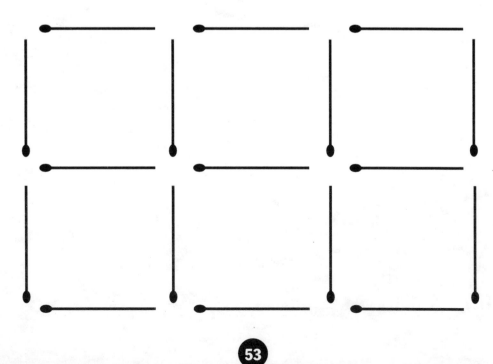

1 On the back seat of a car lies a spirit level. When the car goes round a sharp bend which way will the bubble in the level move, in towards the curb or out towards the middle of the road?

See answer 89.

2 A young couple are about to buy a newly built house. The builder is showing them round and has just reached the bedrooms when he excuses himself and goes to look out the window. With a look of exasperation he flings the window open and yells, 'Green side up, Charlie! Green side up!' He turns back and smiling apologetically explains that he has recently taken on a new lad who is none too bright. Several times during the conversation he flings the window open and shouts the same message to Charlie, but what does it mean?

See answer 8.

3 The little Scots island of Moray boasts the grandly titled Bridge Over the Atlantic (the locals gloss over the fact that, at this point, the Atlantic is only a few feet wide). The bridge is only single track and every morning McLeod the postman drives his van at breakneck speed over the bridge and on to the island. However, every morning Campbell the milkman, who has finished his round, drives his van at similar speed across the bridge as he leaves the island. Neither could ever bring himself to give way so why is there never an accident?

See answer 91.

4 Which is the odd one out: grandfather, sibling, brother-in-law, mother, aunt?

See answer 162.

5 Why is 31 June of such great importance to the islanders of Minki?

See answer 20.

6 Where would you find a system of tunnels 60,000 miles long?

See answer 96.

This is statement which was made at a conference on global warming. 'I can prove that all this fuss about greenhouse gases is nonsense,'stated the scientist boldly. 'Every year the global temperature rises slightly and this is followed about five months later by a rise in the amount of carbon dioxide in the atmosphere. Therefore the carbon dioxide cannot be responsible for the rise in temperature.' Was his logic correct?

See answer 25.

This time you have missed your way in New York. However, the famous places can be located by careful study of the grid. They may be spelt in any direction, not necessarily in a straight line.

BROOKLYN
CITY HALL
UN HQ

LINCOLN CENTER
GREENWICH VILLAGE
FLATIRON BUILDING

BRONX
GRAMERCY PARK
YANKEE STADIUM
HARLEM
LITTLE ITALY
MADISON SQUARE GARDEN

SOHO
CARNEGIE HALL
TIMES SQUARE
CHINA TOWN
GUGGENHEIM

See answer 167.

G	A	C	H	I	N	A	T	O	W	N	U	L	H	V	R	E	G	S	O
Z	R	B	L	T	N	O	S	I	D	A	M	I	Y	X	N	N	O	I	P
R	T	E	U	A	C	S	B	L	D	F	G	T	H	R	T	R	K	M	E
A	L	G	E	P	R	Q	Q	S	A	C	T	T	A	V	Z	Y	X	A	H
R	I	B	Q	N	Z	N	O	U	P	R	C	L	A	C	B	A	L	A	A
S	N	K	A	C	W	R	A	M	A	B	R	E	I	T	A	L	Y	I	L
D	C	G	E	L	E	I	O	N	D	R	O	N	N	O	T	T	I	L	N
G	O	H	A	T	M	N	C	E	W	C	E	T	A	H	S	T	L	U	E
S	L	W	N	A	V	E	S	H	E	Y	G	I	T	H	A	I	S	N	I
S	N	E	A	P	A	I	V	M	N	A	I	M	N	T	H	R	E	H	A
R	C	S	E	G	E	I	I	T	R	T	I	E	S	G	M	O	L	Q	N
C	I	T	Y	E	L	E	Y	O	D	E	N	S	Q	U	A	R	E	E	U
L	L	A	H	L	H	T	O	F	L	A	Y	T	A	D	I	U	M	R	M
L	T	O	A	N	B	R	O	N	X	C	S	P	A	R	K	N	I	S	L
I	K	G	E	E	G	E	T	T	R	I	E	E	K	N	A	Y	N	G	B
L	E	S	O	G	O	D	F	E	R	O	M	L	A	S	T	R	O	O	N
E	I	T	O	G	A	T	M	E	W	R	F	I	A	T	I	I	N	N	G
T	H	H	E	U	S	A	E	B	L	O	I	N	G	T	P	U	Z	B	Z
L	O	E	S	G	R	A	L	D	T	H	E	G	N	I	D	L	I	U	T
T	I	M	E	G	I	T	B	R	O	O	K	L	Y	N	I	S	A	P	A

Match the first name with the surname of these nine famous actors and actresses.

PAUL

NASTASSJA

DEMI

JACOBI

ROBERTS

HUSTON

RYDER

DEREK

HOFFMAN

ARNOLD

MOORE

JULIA

KINSKI

NEWMAN

WINONA

ANJELICA

DUSTIN

SCHWARZENEGGER

See answer 180.

Which is the odd one out?

A   B   C

D   E

See answer 208.

56

1 Put down 24 matches to make a three by three grid of squares. Now remove 8 matches to leave only two squares.

See answer 134.

2 Most match puzzles require only some ingenuity and a little mathematical skill, but this one needs a large dollop of both.

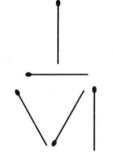

This makes the fraction one sixth. Now add one match so that the result is 1.

See answer 135.

3 Form three squares and two triangles with nine matches.

See answer 136.

1 Farmer Blastem has one of those gas-fuelled bird scaring machines. It lets off an alarming bang once a minute. If he sets it going so that the first bang takes place at 6am, how many times will it have gone off by 7am?

See answer 101.

2 William and Alan are playing with a small plastic ball when it falls down a hole. They find that, no matter how hard they try there is not enough room to get their fingers round the ball to pull it out. 'My dad will kill me,' moans William. 'That ball was a present.' 'Don't worry,' replied his friend, 'there is one sure way to get the ball out.' What did he do?

See answer 57.

1 Another strange but true story. The parish clerk of a Cambridgeshire village received a small parcel from Germany addressed to Mr Alfred White. She checked the telephone directory but could find no one listed under that name. However, when she enquired at the local pub she was told by some of the village old timers that there had been an Alfred White and that, after World War 2, he had married a German girl and settled in Frankfurt. What was in the parcel?

See answer 87.

2 Two little boys come out of a movie. 'I liked the bit where that dinosaur ate all those cave men,' said one. 'Rubbish,' replied his friend, 'it couldn't do it.' 'But that was Tyrannosaurus Rex the most fearsome reptile in the history of the world! Of course it could eat a few lousy cave men.' 'Oh no it couldn't,' insisted his friend with maddening superiority. Who was right?

See answer 98.

3 Dan looked bleakly at the water pump in his car. Kaput! 'I haven't had it more than a couple of years,' he complained to his friend Al. 'You know,' said Al, 'I've got a pump that's lasted 30 years already and I reckon it will keep going for at least twice that long.' Dan was incredulous but Al stuck to his story. What did he mean?

See answer 214.

When the author was a child in Scotland school kids would inflict the following riddle on each other: 'Constantinople is a very big word and if you can't spell it you're a very big dunce!' What was the catch?
See answer 76.

Five couples, each living in a different New York borough, got divorced; and each person then married a partner from one of the other couples. After the change-round no one still lived in the borough where he or she lived before divorcing (i.e., they all moved house). Who is/was married to whom now/previously and where do/did they live? Here are some clues:

1. Mrs Ford (as she is now) lives in the Bronx. Her former husband is Dick, and she isn't Donna.

2. Anna (previously Mrs Smith from Queens) married Joan's former husband and now lives in Brooklyn.

3. Betsy Jones (her current name) was originally from Staten Island; and Jim came from Manhattan before divorcing.

4. Dave and Joan Martin haven't made their new home on Staten Island; and Bobby wasn't the present Mrs Martin's former husband.

Fill in the tables to help you to get the answer.

See answer 171.

Man's New Home / Man's Old Home

	Anna	Betsy	Donna	Joan	Mary	Bronx	Brooklyn	Manhattan	Queens	Staten Island	Bronx	Brooklyn	Manhattan	Queens	Staten Island
Bobby Ford															
Dick Jones															
Jim Lewis															
Dave Martin															
Hank Smith															
Bronx															
Brooklyn															
Manhattan															
Queens															
Staten Island															
Bronx															
Brooklyn															
Manhattan															
Queens															
Staten Island															
Bobby Ford															
Dick Jones															
Jim Lewis															
Dave Martin															
Hank Smith															

Woman's Old Home

Woman's New Home

Woman's Ex-Husband

	Ex-Wife	Ex-Home	New Wife	New Home
Bobby Ford				
Dick Jones				
Jim Lewis				
Dave Martin				
Hank Smith				

What comes next in the sequence?

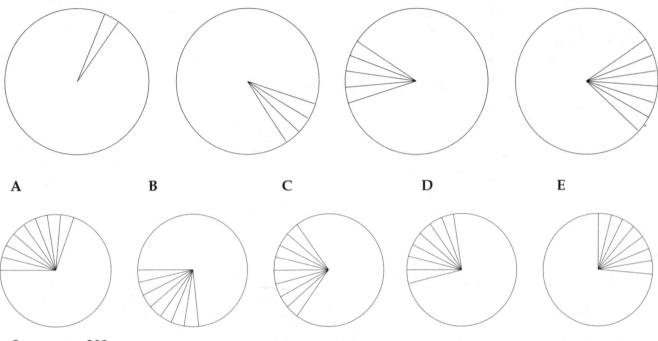

A   B   C   D   E

See answer 209.

What comes next in the sequence?

A   B   C   D   E

See answer 99.

Here's a challenge! Make the sum below work without moving any matches at all.

See answer 148.

Here is a long division sum showing all the working and the result. What could be simpler? The sum works out exactly with no remainder. The slight complication is that all the numbers have been replaced with letters on a random basis. However, one letter always represents the same number. Can you reconstruct the original sum?

See answer 112.

```
          CDEFG
    AB | ADGAAHD
         AJK
         AKA
         AAG
          FA
          JF
          AGH
          AEE
           FD
```

Look at the triangles below. What geometrical shape should logically be placed in the fourth triangle?

See answer 111.

This is a puzzle which is much more fun if you try it on an unsuspecting victim. Take a conical wine glass and two coins, one larger than the other. Place the small coin in the glass first and then the larger. Both coins should lie horizontally with a space between them. You will have to experiment with coins and glasses until you get a combination which will work. Now challenge your victim to remove the smaller coin without touching either of the coins or the glass. If you are particularly sadistic you may even leave a small magnet lying nearby (this will be of no use whatever but may give your victim a considerable amount of frustration trying to work out how to use it). Can you guess how to extract the small coin?

See answer 139.

Which cube below can be made using the diagram on the right:

See answer 189.

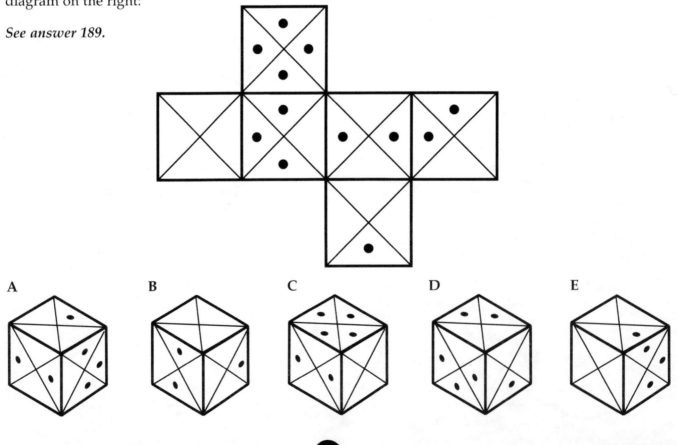

A   B   C   D   E

The annual International Championship cross-country is always a close-run race. This year was no exception with five athletes from various countries having fought their way through to the finals. The last race was to be held over a 10-mile course as shown in the diagram. The race itself was split into four legs, with timekeepers at the end of each leg to record the runners' times. The contestants race from the start A to the end of the first leg at post B, and then on to C and D, finally the sprint across the shortest leg to finish at E. The distances in miles of each of these legs is shown on the course diagram, while the runners' average speeds have been worked out for each leg and then flashed on to the electronic scoreboard, represented in feet per second. (There are 5,280 feet in one mile).

The scoreboard is shown below as it appeared at the end of the race, with all the runners' speeds displayed. Obviously, the first runner past the finishing post won the race. Can you work out their respective times and thus the correct finishing order?

Times in feet/second

RUNNER

	A-B	B-C	C-D	D-E
John	14	12.5	11	13.75
Pierre	13.75	15	8	18.75
Pedro	15	12	8.25	22
Bruce	13	16	8.75	16.5
Ivan	12.75	14	9.75	17.5

See answer 172.

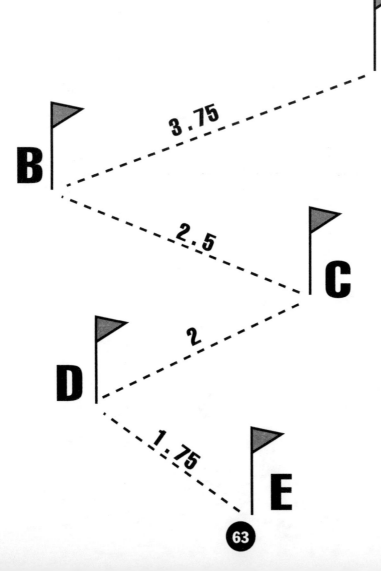

Which is the odd one out?

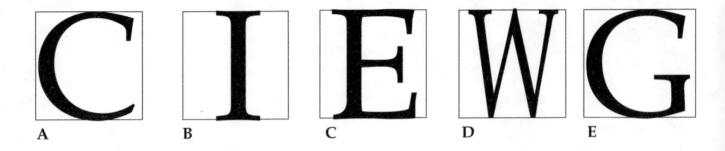

A   B   C   D   E

See answer 61.

Which is the odd one out?

A   B   C

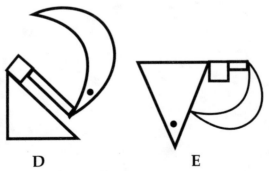

D   E

See answer 216.

1 Queens' College, Cambridge, has a mathematical bridge designed by Sir Isaac Newton. The idea was that all the timbers fitted together without the use of nails, glue or other artificial aids. It worked perfectly until some bright spark decided to take it to bits for refurbishment. They eventually got it back together but only by using hefty metal bolts to hold it. Could you design a similar bridge using a couple of dozen matchsticks? Your bridge need have no sides, it will be a flat object which can be raised in the middle so that it bends without breaking.

See answer 140.

2 How would you make a tower of twenty matchboxes which you could hold in one hand without it falling over. No glue, sticky tape, etc, is allowed - just guile, cunning and general sneakiness!

See answer 137.

3 Take a matchbox and pull it apart. Then put the parts together as shown in the diagram. Now turn the whole thing upside down. You may hold the case by a finger and thumb only but you must not touch the tray at all.

See answer 138.

1 This one is a true story. A racing cyclist came off his bike at speed, fell awkwardly and broke nearly all the bones in his right hand. After hospital treatment the hand was much improved and, one day, a consultant invited a group of students to consider the case. 'This man,' he said, 'is not a professional cyclist. He works as a graphic designer. How long after the accident do you think he was able to return to work?' The students examined x-rays of the hand taken just after the accident and gave a variety of opinions. What would your answer have been?

See answer 92.

2 Many authors have written entertainingly about time travel but what would actually happen if you could be taken out of time for, say, five seconds and then returned to exactly the same spot?

See answer 72.

The numbers in this calculation have been replaced by letters. All the numbers from 0-9 have been used, and by telling you that R=2 we hope to have given you enough information to keep you down to one solution. Each letter represents the same number every time it appears. Can you work out the original calculation?

See answer 173.

 is to as 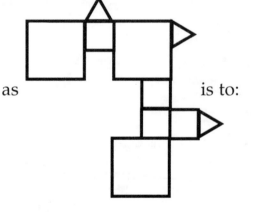 is to:

See answer 210.

A   B   C   D   E

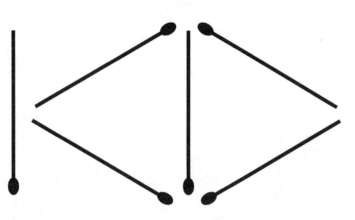

Have a look at these diagrams. Can you work out what is opposite the blank face of cube number 4?

See answer 67.

Lay six matches in a fish pattern as above: Now try to make eight equilateral triangles by moving three matches.

See answer 142.

Use six straight lines to divide the diagram into seven sections containing 1, 2, 3, 4, 5, 6, and 7 stars respectively. The lines always touch one edge of the box, but not necessarily two.

See answer 179.

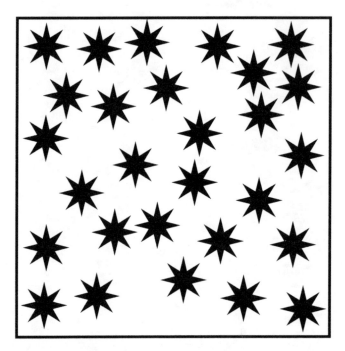

Which of the following completes a diamond when fitted with the diagram below:

See answer 223.

A   B

CC   D   E

1 Dick is getting dressed for an important dinner party with the boss and his wife. They are outside in the car waiting to take him to the restaurant. He is already running late when suddenly, disaster! There's a power cut. He hasn't yet put on his socks. He knows that in the drawer there are a dozen pairs of black socks and an equal number of navy ones. What is the smallest number of socks he must take out of the drawer to avoid the embarrassment of mismatched socks?

See answer 103.

2 Dave and Anne moved into their new home and then went to the DIY store to make an important purchase. 'How much is one?' asked Dave. '$3,' came the reply. 'What about 20?' 'That'll cost you $6.' 'OK, well we need 2042.' What were Dave and Anne buying and how much did it cost them?

See answer 218.

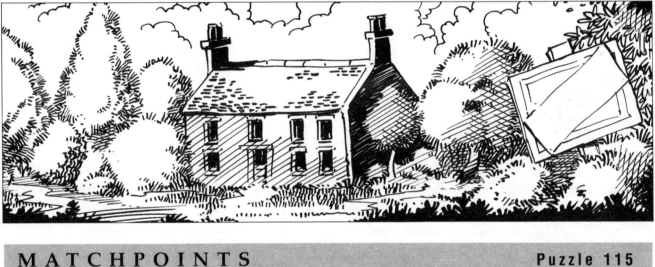

This is a sum using Roman numerals made out of matches. Move one match to make the sum correct.

See answer 145.

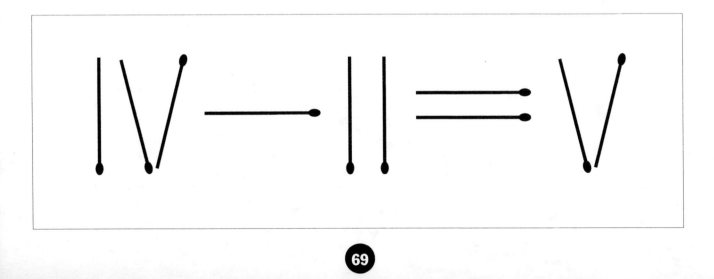

Which one of the five pieces shown correctly fits into the vacant section of the grid?

See answer 175.

Use five straight lines to divide this square into seven sections containing 1, 2, 3, 4, 5, 6, and 7 spots. The lines always touch one edge of the box, but not necessarily two.

See answer 178.

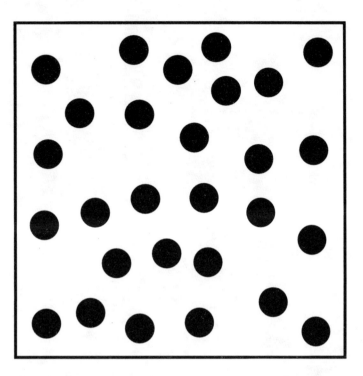

Which is the odd one out?

A   B   C   D   E

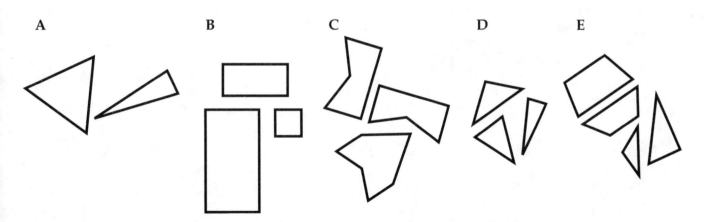

See answer 224.

This simple calculation uses Roman numerals made from matches. Move two matches to make the sum work.

See answer 146.

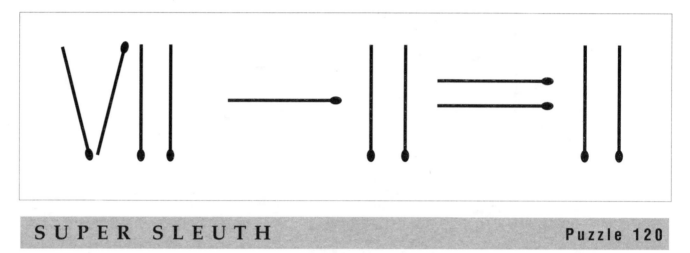

1 Once, in India, a queen owned two horses and used them to help destroy a neighbouring king. There was a hard fought battle in which all the king's men were killed. When the battle was over the victors and the vanquished all lay side by side in the same place. Explain.

See answer 186.

2 What does nobody want but nobody wants to lose?

See answer 220.

DEAD END

E-MAIL MESSAGE

From: Chief of Police O'Malley
To: Robotic Tracer XJ -256   **Location:** New York
Dateline: 4 August 2210   **Security Code:** 10

Yesterday evening at 10pm the President's daughter was kidnapped. A news blackout was immediately enforced but, in spite of the best efforts of all law enforcement agencies, no trace was found. In the last hour a message was received from the kidnapper. A transcript follows.

"My name is Alan Timms and, until recently, I worked as a scientist in the Department of Defense. In spite of my genius and the many brilliant ideas that I have offered for the defense of this country I have never received the recognition that was my due. Again and again I have been passed over in favor of some blue-eyed boy with a gift for self advancement. Six months ago I discovered that I was dying. So I made a decision. If I was not to go down in history as one of the world's great scientists, then I would be the greatest criminal of all time. I have now kidnapped the President's daughter. There is no need to look for her, she is to be found in a deserted office block marked on the map you will find with this note. I am with her. However, before you come blundering in here with your police and your National Guard, there are things you should know. The girl is locked inside a machine of my own devising. She is floating in a pressurised bath of nutrients and can safely remain in suspension for as long as necessary.

However, if any attempt is made to release her a cocktail of deadly nerve gases will be introduced into the chamber and she will die an agonising death right in front of your eyes. I have devised a little game and, if you want the girl back, you will agree to play it. All around New York I have hidden a series of clues. You will select an agent to follow my trail and solve every riddle I have set. If your agent can follow the correct path and find the correct code you will be able to open the machine and release the girl. But you will have to be fast. From the moment your agent starts you have only two hours."

Tracer XJ-256, the map he mentions can be viewed on your telescreen. As you solve each puzzle you will be given the location of the next. Your country depends on you. Good luck.

1 POLICE STATION

All the objects in this grid have a numerical value. The totals of the values for each row, column and one of the diagonals have been inserted. One figure is missing and it is up to you to find it. When you have the solution subtract 44 and then go to the location of that number.

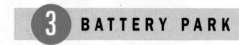

3 BATTERY PARK

This is a road map of part of New York City. You can see the routes taken by four drivers A, B, C, D. The side of each square is one mile long. The speed of driver A is 20 mph. Driver B drives at 22 mph. Driver C drives at 25 mph. Driver D drives at 27 mph. Which car(s) reach a shaded circle first and in what time? When you have the time in minutes subtract 13 and go to the location of that number.

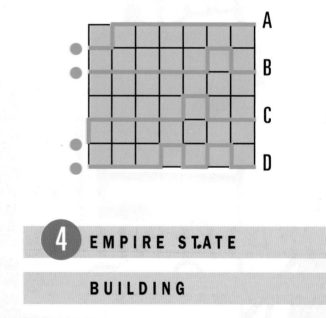

2 EAST VILLAGE

You are supplied with three darts which you throw at the board. Assume that each time you throw them all the darts hit the board. How many different ways are there of scoring 12? When you have the answer add 23 and go to that location.

4 EMPIRE STATE

BUILDING

The figures in the diagram are linked in some way. Find the figure which should go in the middle of the third triangle. When you have it add 18 and go to the location of that number.

If your answer is a circle, go to location **22**   If your answer is a triangle, go to location **9**
If your answer is a rectangle, go to location **13**   If your answer is a square, go to location **10**

5 YANKEE STADIUM

Look at the three sets of scales. Each object has a certain weight. Which object is needed to balance the last set of scales?

6 GRAND CENTRAL STATION

This signpost shows you the distances to a number of New York locations. The distances shown are calculated from numerical values placed upon the letters in each name. Find the distance to Grand Central Station. When you know the answer subtract 47 and go to the location of that number.

RIVERSIDE PARK	47
TIMES SQUARE	39
HARLEM	22
GRAND CENTRAL STATION	?

7 STATUE OF LIBERTY

The numbers around the squares are linked in some way. Find the correct number to go in the middle of the third square. When you have it subtract 134 and go to the location of the number you now have.

8 FIREARMS COMPLEX

The numbers on the diagram have a relationship to each other. Can you find out what it is and thus fill in the missing number? When you have done it subtract 83 and go to the next location.

Diagram numbers:
10 6   5   6
11   16 5   7
8 27   63 8
9 56   ?   9
   30 60
7   3
   5   1   8   2

9 ROCKEFELLER CENTER

All the objects in this diagram have a numerical value. Find the number which will correctly replace the question mark. When you have it divide it by 4. The result will take you to the next location.

?
59
78
57

77   73   44   60   73

10 SOHO

Find the missing letter in this series. If your answer is G, go to 2. If your answer is H, go to 11. If your answer is K, go to 26. If your answer is L, go to 35.

C F H ? M

Flip this figure over and rotate it. Which of the figures below do you get? If your answer is A, go to 21. If your answer is B, go to 12. If your answer is C, go to 30. If your answer is D, go to 6.

The numbers you see here are related in some way. Crack the logic and find the missing number. When you have it subtract 30 and go to your next location.

13 BROOKLYN BRIDGE

Here is a signpost in which the distances are all related to the letters used. Find the distance to China Town, subtract 29, and continue to the next location.

SOHO	18
TRIBECA	29
LITTLE ITALY	42
CHINA TOWN	?

14 MANHATTAN

These Roman numerals are connected by some strange logic. Find the missing one, add XVI, and go on to the next location.

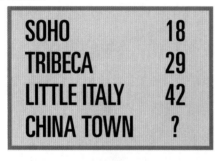

15 HARLEM

This wall is covered with graffiti. The words are connected in some kind of series. Who does Oliver love? If you think it's Lauren, go to location 16. If you think it's Nicole, go to location 3. If you think it's Latoya, go to location 29. If you think it's Urania, go to location 10. If you think it's Kimberley, go to location 26.

Aaron ♥ Crystal

Franco ♥ Jessica

Oliver ♥

Lauren, Nicole, Latoya, Urania, Kimberley.

⑯ AIRPORT

Find the missing number. When you have it add 28 and continue on your way.

3	7	5	5
6	6	6	2
7	11	1	1
8	3	4	?

⑰ NATIONAL HEALTH COMPLEX

These letters are an anagram of a place in New York. Unscramble the words and look up the number of that place on the map. Subtract 23 and go to a new location.

SNYBTIOGKHRHELO

⑱ MAXIMUM SECURITY PRISON

Try to find the logic which connects these numbers. When you find the missing one subtract 135 and go to your new location.

? 84 168
189
126 105

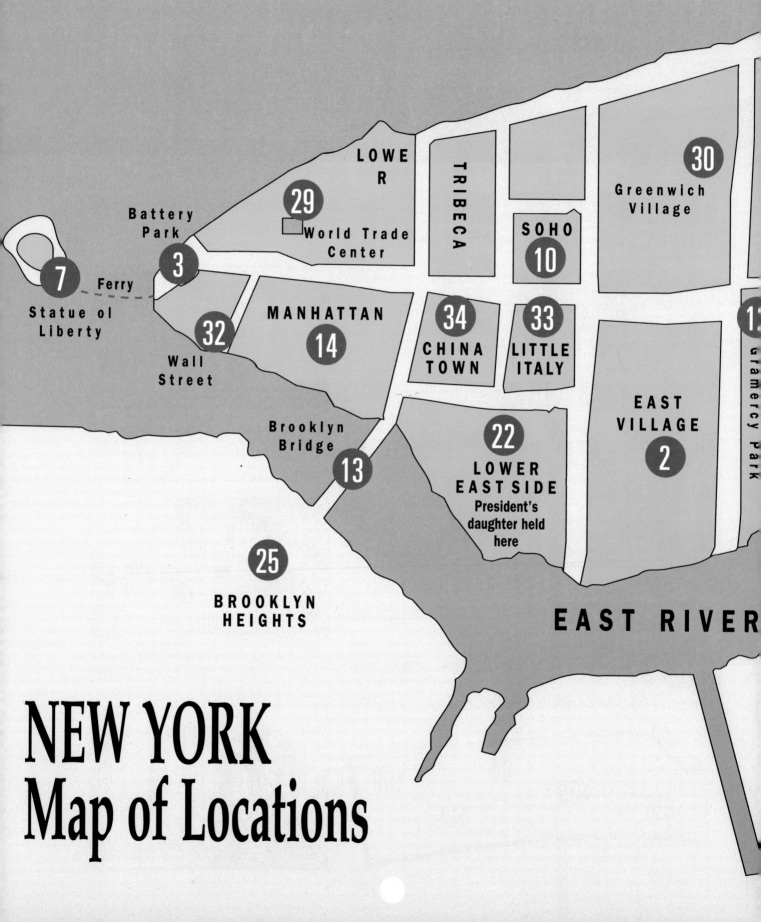

HUDSON

LOWER

29

Battery
Park

3

7

Ferry

Statue ol
Liberty

32

Wall
Street

MANHATTAN

14

TRIBECA

SOHO

10

34

CHINA
TOWN

33

LITTLE
ITALY

30

Greenwich
Village

World Trade
Center

Brooklyn
Bridge

13

22

LOWER
EAST SIDE

President's
daughter held
here

EAST
VILLAGE

2

Gramercy Park

25

BROOKLYN
HEIGHTS

EAST RIVER

NEW YORK
Map of Locations

⑲ UPPER WEST SIDE

Look at the scales. Each object has a numerical value. Try to work out which object is needed to balance the last set of scales. If your answer is a circle, go to 14. If your answer is a rectangle, go to 29. If your answer is a triangle, go to 31. If your answer is a square, go to 32.

⑳ N.Y. PUBLIC LIBRARY

Look at the triangles. Work out what the missing figure is, subtract 17 and continue on your way.

㉑ MAIN PRISON

Here is another anagram of a New York place name. When you have worked it out look up the number of that place on the map and subtract 6 to get your next location.

EVLGRENG
AWHCLEII

LOWER EAST SIDE

The numbers surrounding the squares are connected in some way. Work out the logic and supply the missing number. When you have it subtract 14 and find your new destination.

23

ZOO

Again a number is missing. Unravel the logic to find the missing number then subtract 115 and go to the new location.

24

METROPOLITAN

MUSEUM OF ART

Here is another number grid. Replace the question mark with a number, add 19 and go to the next location.

25 BROOKLYN HEIGHTS

Look at the building facing you. The height of the building opposite, measured in yards, is 2 times the square of 5, multiplied by the square root of 36. When you have the solution subtract 284 and go to the next location.

26 CASINO

You need to choose two figures to complete the pattern. Which do you choose. If your choice is HB, go to location 18. If you choose EF, go to location 29. If you choose AG, go to 25. If you choose DC, go to 15. If you choose DH, go to 16.

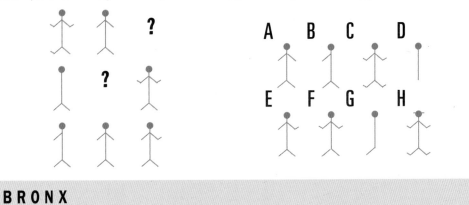

27 BRONX

Find the figure which goes next in the series. If you choose A go to 23. If you choose B, go to 28. If you choose C, go to 13. If you choose D, go to 11.

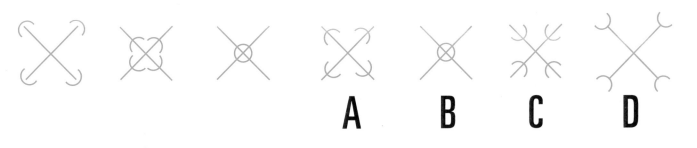

28 RIVERSIDE PARK

Find the missing number. When you have it add 17 and go to the next location.

29 WORLD TRADE CENTER

Look at the diagrams and find the missing letter. Add 10 to the value of that letter and go to the next location.

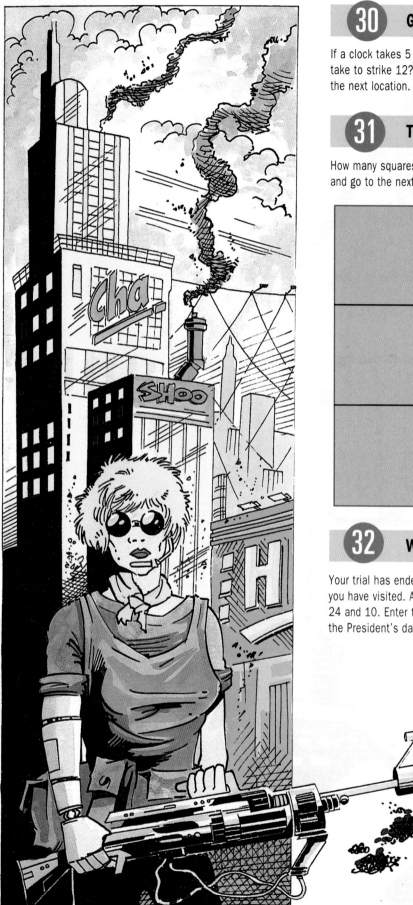

30 GREENWICH VILLAGE

If a clock takes 5 seconds to strike six, how many seconds will it take to strike 12? Subtract 4 from your answer and continue to the next location.

31 TIMES SQUARE

How many squares of any size are there in this figure? Add 15 and go to the next location.

32 WALL STREET

Your trial has ended. You should now have a list of the location you have visited. Add together all the numbers between locations 24 and 10. Enter this total into the computer and, if it is correct, the President's daughter will be relased. Or will she?

What number is half the value of a third of 102? When you discover the answer, add 1 and go to the location of that number.

(34) CHINATOWN

Find the missing number. When you have it, go to that location.

1	2	5	7
47	55	62	11
41	79	71	?
34	29	23	19

(35) UN HQ

There is a curious logic to this series. Can you replace the question mark with the final number? (The answer is right before your eyes!) When you have the number, divide it by 2.

5 2 1 7 5 2 4 6 3 3 7 3 8 4 4 3 5 ?

ANSWERS

1. Police Station: 61–44=17. **2. East Village:** 12+23=35. **3. Battery Park:** A and C, 24–13=11. **4. Empire State Building:** 2+18=20. **5. Yankee Stadium:** Triangle, go to 9. **6. Grand Central Station:** 70–47=23. **7. Statue of Liberty:** 162–134=28. **8. Firearms Complex:** 11x8=88-83=5. **9. Rockefeller Center:** 60÷4=15. **10. Soho:** K, go to 26. **11. Turtle Bay:** A, go to 21. **12. Gramercy Park:** 36–30=6. **13. Brooklyn Bridge:** 33–29=4. **14. Manhattan:** 14+16=30. **15. Harlem:** Urania, go to 10. **16. Airport:** 5+28=33. **17. National Health Complex:** Brooklyn Heights = 25. 25–23=2. **18. Maximum Security Prison:** 147–135=12. **19. Upper West Side:** Triangle, go to 31. **20. N.Y. Public Library:** 36–17=19. **21. Main Prison:** Greenwich Village = 30. 30–6=24. **22. Lower East Side:** 22–14=8. **23. Zoo:** 147–115=32. **24. Metropolitan Museum of Art:** 8+19=27. **25. Brooklyn Heights:** 300–284=16. **26. Casino:** AG, go to 25. **27. Bronx:** C, go to 13. **28. Riverside Park:** 5+17=22. **29. World Trade Center:** x=29+10=34. **30. Greenwich Village:** 11–4=7. **31. Times Square:** 14+15=29.33. **33. Little Italy:** 17+1=18. **34. Chinatown:** 14. **35. UN HQ:** 6÷2=3.

To release the President's daughter, the number you need to enter into the computer is 349.

Insert one of the four basic mathematical
signs in each space to complete the sum,
starting from the top. One sign is used
twice, the rest once.

+ – X ÷

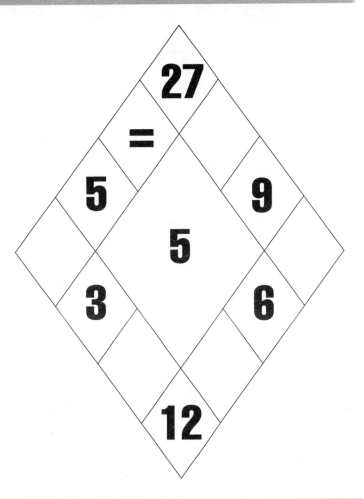

See answer 124.

What letter does the question mark represent ?

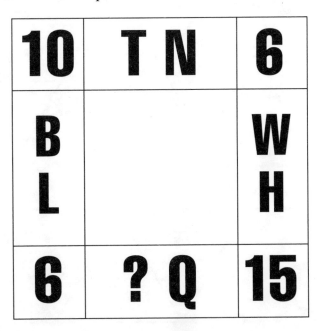

See answer 106.

How much is the question mark worth?

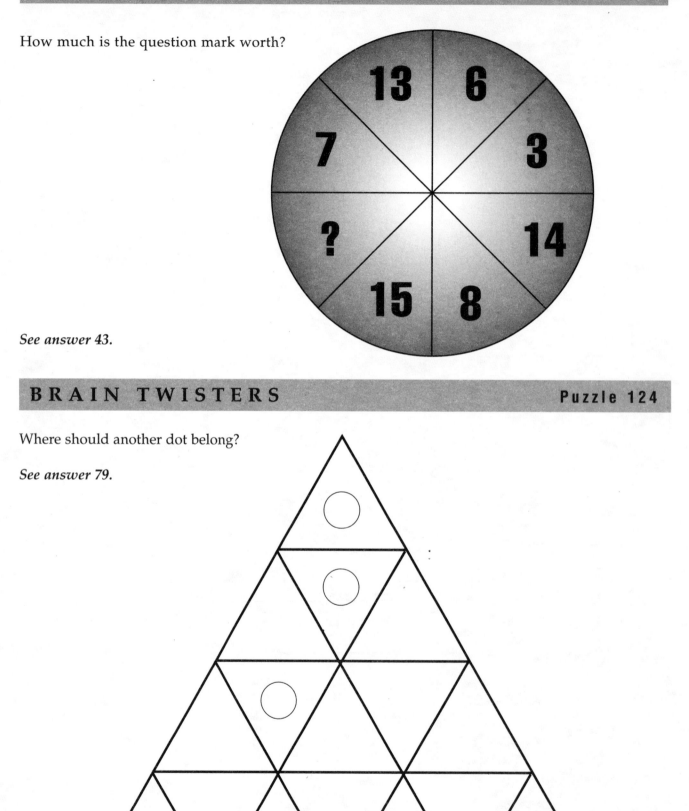

See answer 43.

Where should another dot belong?

See answer 79.

Which one of the five pieces shown correctly fits
into the vacant section of the grid?

See answer 176.

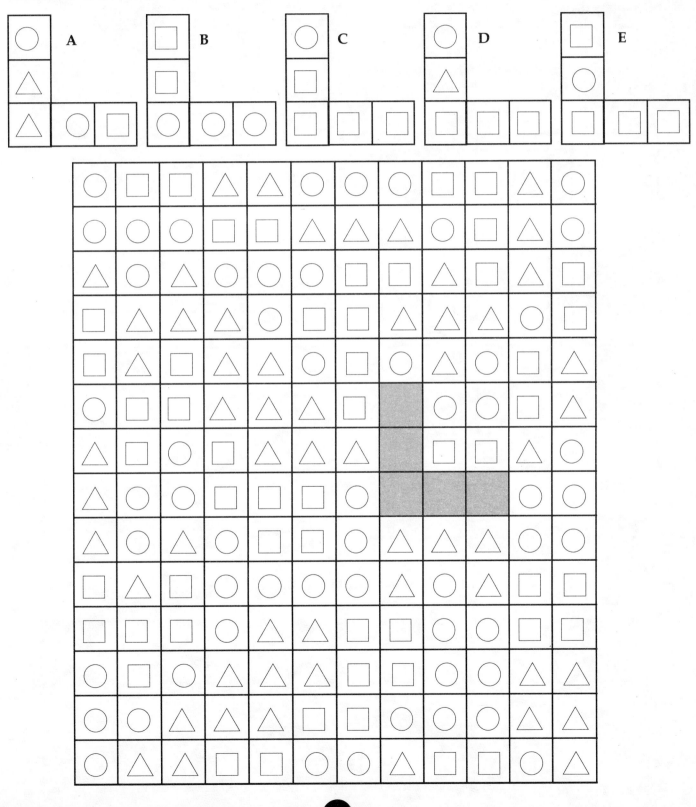

Five colleagues set off for work each day in their vehicles. Work out who drives what and how long they each drive to work.

1. Pauline drives twice as long as the estate car and a quarter of the time that Olivia has to drive in her saloon car.

2. Neville and Pauline drive 60 minutes between them but Neville has five times the travel time as Pauline.

3. The convertible travels half as long as Neville while Lynda takes five times longer than Martin.

4. The sports car has the longest journey and the van has a quarter of the trip of the saloon.

See answer 177.

	Convertible	Estate	Saloon	Sports	Van	5 minutes	10 minutes	25 minutes	40 minutes	50 minutes
Lynda										
Martin										
Neville										
Olivia										
Pauline										
5 minutes					
10 minutes					
25 minutes					
40 minutes					
50 minutes					

Name	Type of Vehicle	Time
Lynda		
Martin		
Neville		
Olivia		
Pauline		

Which is the odd one out?

A   B   C

D   E

See answer 226.

76

1 Vinyl records are not used much any more but, strangely they still seem perfect for puzzle setters. An old fashioned 78 has a diameter of 12 ins. The outside border is $1/2$ in wide and the distance from there to the central hole is $5^1/2$ ins. If you put the stylus down at the very edge of the playing area how far will the needle have travelled by the time the music stops? You may assume that there are 83 grooves to the inch.

See answer 110.

2 The Bacillus subtilis bacterium reproduces simply by splitting in two. It can do this every 20 minutes. Given perfect conditions how many offspring do you think one organism could produce in eight hours?

See answer 86.

A party of Mensa members was being given a guided tour of the Clocks and Watches Gallery. 'I bet you can't tell me which timepiece has the fewest moving parts,' said the Curator. 'A sundial' bellowed the intellectually gifted ones. 'OK,' said the slightly peeved Curator, 'which timepiece has the most moving parts?' There was a prolonged silence. What was the answer?

See answer 108.

Which of the following cubes below can be made using the flat
one shown here ?

A   B   C   D   E

See answer 21.

Which is the odd one out?

4   **15**   **9**   **12**   **5**
A   B   C   D   E

8   **30**   **18**   **24**   **10**
F   G   H   I   J

See answer 229.

HEADSCRATCHERS Puzzle 132

In an orchestra there is something which is neither blown, bowed, plucked or struck but without which the others could not play. What is it?

See answer 128.

MATCHPOINTS Puzzle 133

Remove three matches from this sum to make the equation correct.

See answer 147.

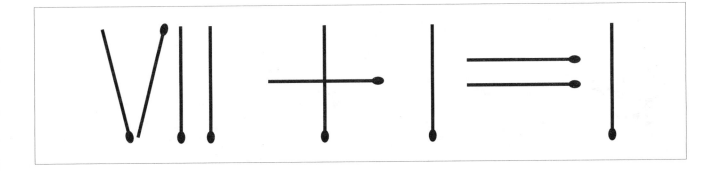

SUPER SLEUTH Puzzle 134

1 How many times can you subtract the number 2 from the number 46?

See answer 24.

2 Eddie has a reputation for being, let's say, economical. There are two girls he's interested in and he has the chance to take them both to the movies. His problem is that he wants a good deal. Will it be cheaper for him to take them both together, or should he take them separately?

See answer 52.

To which of the following can a dot be added to meet the conditions of the drawing on the right?

A   B   C   D   E

See answer 212.

is to   as   is to:

A   B   C   D   E

See answer 225.

Which one of the five pieces shown correctly fits
into the vacant section of the grid?

See answer 174.

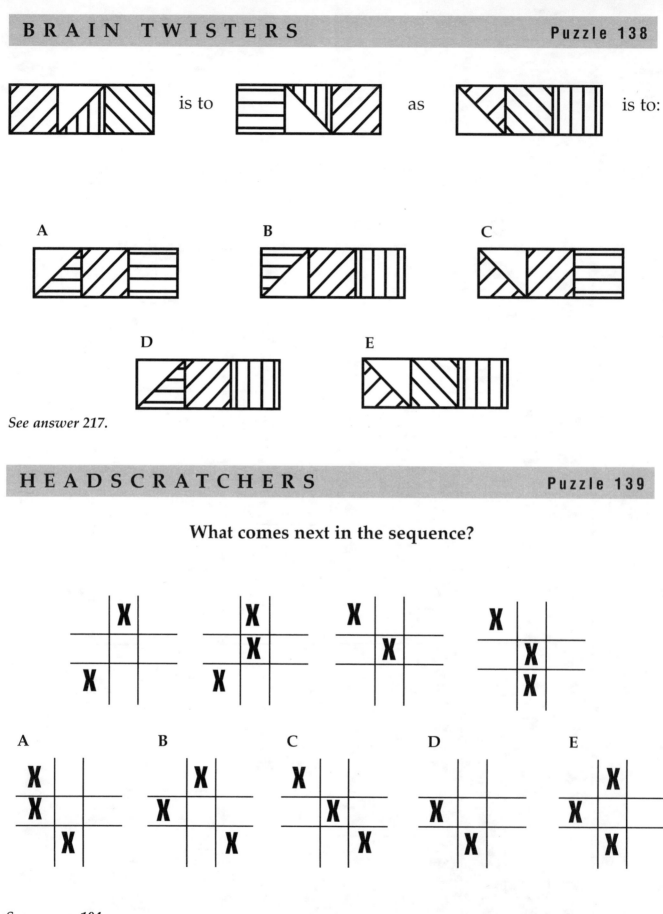

See answer 217.

What comes next in the sequence?

A   B   C   D   E

See answer 104.

Which of the following sets of triangles can be used to make a square?

See answer 109.

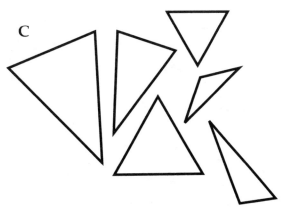

w is to **n** as **d** is to:

A   B   C   D   E

See answer 75.

What comes next in the following sequence:

See answer 227.

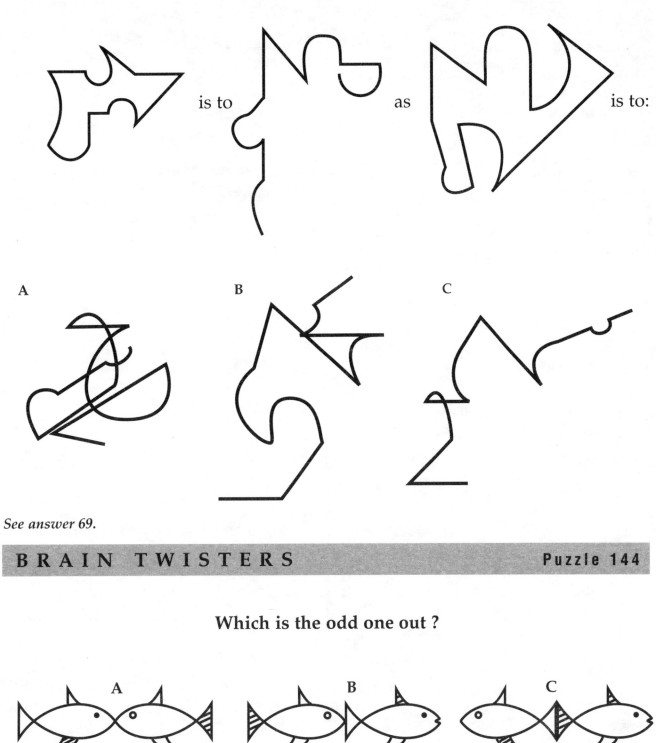

is to   as   is to:

A   B   C

See answer 69.

Which is the odd one out ?

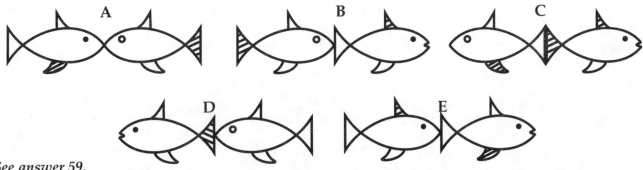

See answer 59.

1 Frieda drove her husband Andy to Chicago airport and watched him climb aboard the 7.15 flight for London. As she arrived home she heard that the 7.15 London flight had crashed on take-off and there were no survivors. Strangely she got on with preparing an evening meal for her and her husband. Why?

See answer 74.

2 Dan and his best friend Dave were out fishing when they noticed a shark circling their dinghy. Whenever they tried to move the boat the shark would barge into it nearly causing it to capsize. 'Never mind,' said Dan, 'if we wait long enough it'll get tired and while it's asleep we can sneak away.' Was this good advice?

See answer 107.

3 Two fathers and two sons went into a bar to have a Friday night drink together. They spent $15. Each spent the same amount. How much did each man spend?

See answer 95.

1 Use 16 matches to make this figure. Now remove four matches to leave four triangles.

See answer 143.

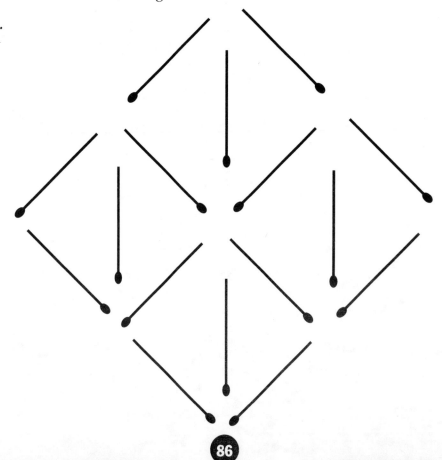

Which of the following fills the gap?

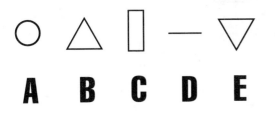

A   B   C   D   E

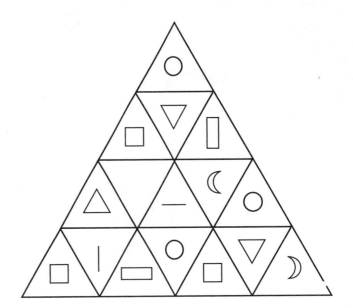

See answer 222.

How much is the question mark worth?

See answer 73.

How much is the question mark worth?

?	HEY	10
H P Z		A N O
12	IUA	11

See answer 204.

Each pattern is worth a certain value. The values are 3 consecutive odd numbers under 10. With 6 segments, there are 6 values, with the total sum being 16. What is each pattern worth?

See answer 105.

Insert one of the four basic mathematical signs in each space to complete the sum, starting from the top. One sign is used twice, the rest once.

$+ \quad - \quad X \quad \div$

See answer 97.

How much is the question mark worth?

See answer 132.

Insert one of the four basic mathematical
signs in each space to complete the sum,
starting from the top. One sign is used twice,
the rest once. Each letter represents its
position in the alphabet, where A = 1 and Z
= 26.

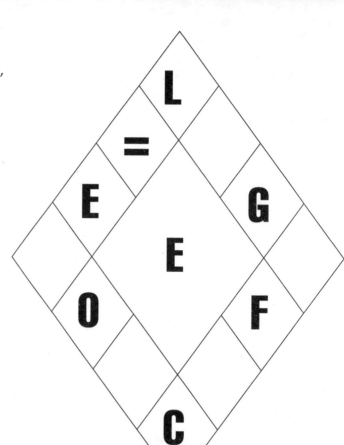

See answer 121.

What shape is missing and where should it go?

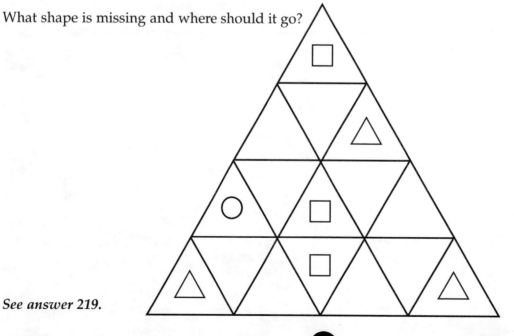

See answer 219.

How much is the question mark worth?

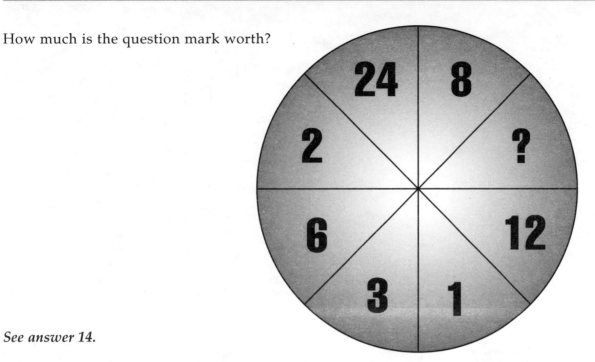

See answer 14.

What letter does the question mark represent ?

?	725	M
1 3 9		4 7 2
I	846	N

See answer 122.

The pattern in each segment is worth either 2, 4, 6 or 8 points. The total value of the circle's 10 segments is 44. What is each pattern worth?

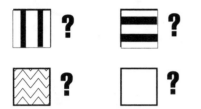 ?   ▬ ?

▨ ?   □ ?

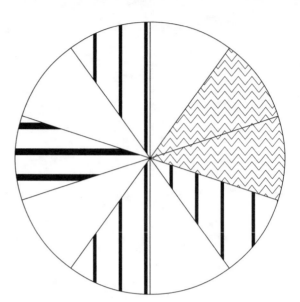

See answer 113.

How much is the question mark worth?

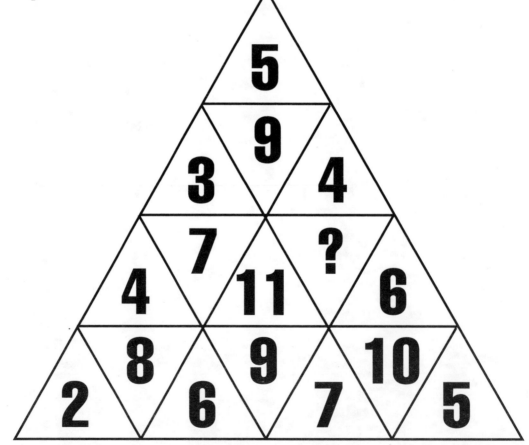

See answer 32.

Insert one of the four basic mathematical signs in each space to complete the sum, starting from the top. One sign is used twice, the rest once.

+ – X ÷

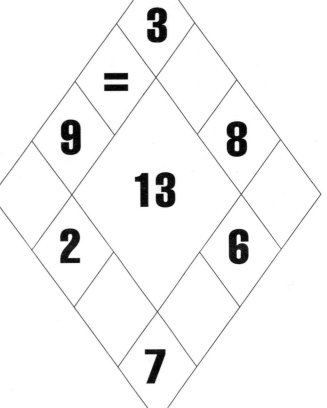

See answer 70.

The values of the patterns are 3 consecutive even numbers under 10, with the total of 20 being the sum of the segment values. How much is each pattern worth?

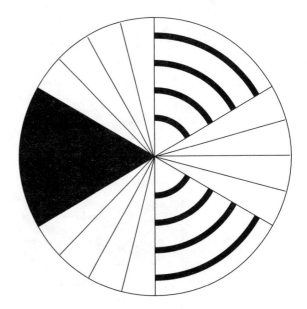

See answer 93.

How much is the question mark worth?

See answer 40.

1	6	6
7	8	56
9	7	?

What letter does the question mark represent ?

44	QLA	30
?OY		HTU
33	IFR	49

See answer 100.

How much is the question mark worth?

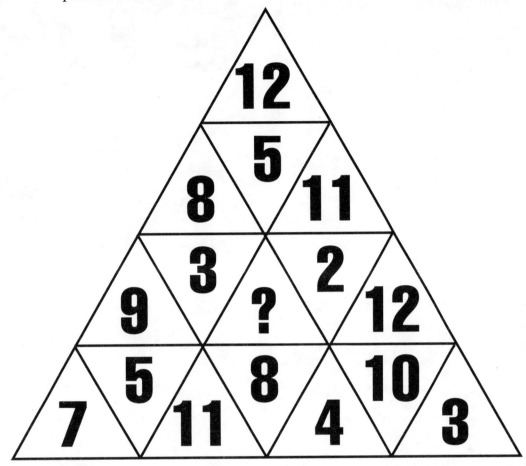

See answer 90.

How much is the question mark worth?

See answer 159.

How much is the question mark worth?

See answer 152.

Insert one of the four basic mathematical signs in each space to complete the sum, starting from the top. One sign is used twice, the rest once. Each letter represents its position in the alphabet, where A = 1 and Z = 26.

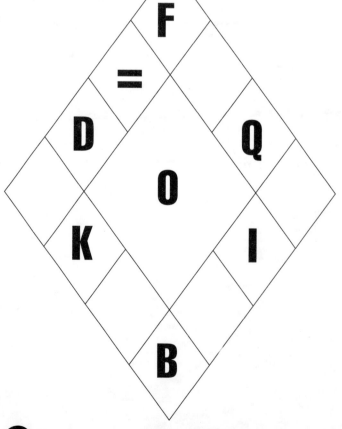

See answer 115.

How much is the question mark worth?

A	B	C	D	E
5	3	7	23	33
12	2	2	12	16
8	9	10	56	114
6	4	8	35	45
5	7	6	40	?

See answer 228.

Each pattern is worth either 1, 3, 5 or 7 points. The total value is 34. What is each pattern worth?

See answer 155.

ANSWERS

Answer 1
The Nile.

Answer 2
He isn't dead.

Answer 3
A clock with a second hand.

Answer 4
Wait until dusk when the frogs climb out of the water and go hunting.

Answer 5
He held it 2.5 metres (eight feet) above the floor. True, it fell two metres without breaking but, on hitting the floor, it smashed to smithereens!

Answer 6
The frog will never reach the edge.

Answer 7
Place the first egg in the middle. Every time your opponent places an egg you must place one diametrically opposite his. That way you will always place the final egg.

Answer 8
Charlie is in the garden laying turf for a lawn.

QUICK WIT Answer 9
He was a tourist looking for a souvenir and shot the sergeant with a camera.

Answer 10
All except February.

Answer 11
If hyperbolic acid could eat its way through anything, you could not put it in a flask.

QUICK WIT Answer 12
Captains don't lead battalions.

Answer 13
D.

Answer 14
4. Products of pairs of numbers facing each other equals 24.

Answer 15
The wife was heavily pregnant. While her husband was away she went into labour and had twins which, being a resourceful woman, she delivered herself.

Answer 16
He remembered too late why he had come in the first place – the electric window winder on the driver's door was broken and the window was open.

Answer 17
Polar Bears are only found in the Arctic (North Pole).

Answer 18
Candles for birthday cakes.

Answer 19
He stuck a small piece of sticky tape to the balloon and pushed the pin through the tape.

Answer 20
The date, like the islanders, does not exist.

Answer 21
E.

Answer 22
E. In all other cases the letters, if reflected along an imaginary vertical line, still form a letter.

ANSWERS

Answer 23
No, they would be moonquakes.

Answer 24
Only once. After that you are subtracting from 44, 42, etc.

QUICK WIT Answer 25
No. He was confusing himself by thinking in terms of years (a purely arbitrary measure of time). What was happening was that the carbon dioxide level rose and then, some months later, so did the temperature.

QUICK WIT Answer 26
The third horse was a clothes horse.

Answer 27
The flat was in the spare.

SUPER SLEUTH Answer 28
The dead man was a mechanic. He had been servicing the car while the owner went on holiday. While he was working on the car the jack gave way and the car fell on him.

Answer 29
1. Starting with 64, subtract 1, 2, 4, 8, 16, 32, missing a number each time and working in a clockwise direction.

Answer 30
A door.

Answer 31
It was an adult movie and Dave's uncle is only ten years old.

Answer 32
8. Sequence of adding 2, subtracting 1, in the pattern followed by working round the triangle in the 2, 4, 3, 5, 4, 6, 5, 7, 6, 8, etc. pattern.

Answer 33
Dr Bicuspid. Since these are the only two dentists in town it is certain they do each other's dental work. Therefore Dr Molar must be responsible for the poor state of his partner's teeth and should be avoided.

QUICK WIT Answer 34
He had loaded the sacks with sand so they would actually get heavier after they had been in water.

Answer 35
Bartok, Delius, Mahler, Mozart, Puccini, Purcell Rachmaninov, Rimsky-Korsakov, Sibelius, Schubert.

Answer 36
As many times as you like. And the answer will always be 14.491297!

Answer 37
The wind is coming from the north but the road is going to the north.

Answer 38
2:1 on.

Answer 39
The truck was a car transporter and the cars were its cargo.

Answer 40
63. In each row, the product of the first 2 numbers equals the third.

Answer 41
B. Rotate the figure 90 degrees clockwise and reflect the curved lines.

Answer 42
C. In all other cases, the biggest shape is also the smallest.

Answer 43

18. Sum of the pairs of numbers facing each other equals 21.

Answer 44

E. The value of letter given by position in the alphabet is added together. An even answer should give a triangle, an odd answer a circle.

Answer 45

It is true that Sue and Hannah are sisters, but they are not each other's sisters.

Answer 46

So were the other half.

Answer 47

T (All the letters can be reversed laterally and remain the same).

Answer 48

C. The minute hand moves forward five minutes and the hour hand moves forward three hours.

Answer 49

Two (one on each side, each going in ever decreasing circles round to the hole in the middle).

Answer 130

Answer 60

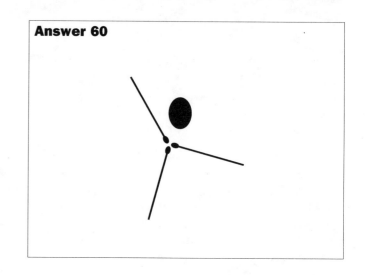

Answer 50

Frozen sea water contains much less salt than it does when liquid. By melting lumps of ice from the sea there would be ample water for the crew to drink.

Answer 51

Jim had retired as captain and was watching on TV. The papers compared the team's current miserable performance with it's fame under Jim's captaincy.

Answer 52

Two girls at the same time would mean buying three tickets. One girl twice would require four tickets as he buys for himself on both occasions.

Answer 53

'I've run away from home but I'm not old enough to cross the road myself!'

Answer 54

Neither – fish are cold-blooded.

Answer 55

You saw the explosion on TVs in a shop window.

Answer 56

A.

Answer 67

 is opposite the blank face.

Answer 57
He got a bucket of water which he emptied into the hole to float the ball to the surface.

Answer 58
Black = 8; Speckled = 9.

Answer 59
C. When fish face outwards mouth should be open.

Answer 60
See diagram on Page 100.

Answer 61
D. All the others touch the sides in two separate places, but this one touches the sides in four places.

Answer 62
A whip.

Answer 63
Because 1884 is one more than 1883.

Answer 64
'Are you dead?'

Answer 65
No one. The barber was the mayor's wife.

Answer 66
The hours move back 3, 4, 5, and 6 hours. The minutes move forward 4, 8, 16, and 32 minutes. The seconds move back 1, 2, 3, and 4 seconds. The time on the fifth watch should be 21.14.51.

Answer 67
See box above.

Answer 68
4. The answer depends upon the number of the four-sided figures within which the number lies.

Answer 143

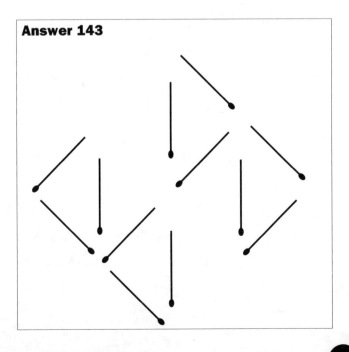

Answer 112

```
              86374
    19 1641106
       152
          121
          114
             71
             57
            140
            133
              76
```

Answer 133

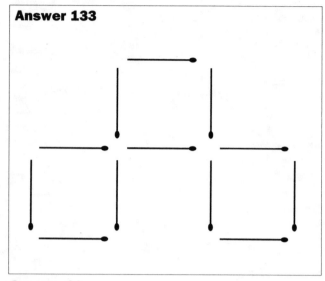

Answer 69
C. Curves are reflected. Horizontal and vertical lines interchange and diagonals go in opposite directions.

Answer 70
$3 \times 8 \div 6 + 7 \times 2 - 9 = 13$.

Answer 71
An armchair.

Answer 72
You would die. During the five seconds of your absence the earth would have travelled a considerable distance and you would be stranded in airless outer space.

Answer 73
120. Working clockwise starting from 9, each 2 adjacent small numbers are multiplied together to get the adjacent total.

Answer 74
Andy was a member of the ground crew. He climbed aboard the plane, serviced it and climbed right down again.

Answer 75
D. The vertical mirror image of w is m, the letter before n. The vertical mirror image of d is p, the letter before q.

Answer 76
It is spelt IT.

Answer 77
Fold the postcard and cut. See design on Page 105.

Answer 78
D. In all other cases the number of cross pieces on top of each vertical line is multiplied by the number of cross pieces on the bottom. All give even answers apart from D.

Answer 79
Penultimate triangle on the bottom row. Sequence, starting from the top and working from left to right, of dot, miss 1 triangle, dot, miss 2, dot, miss 3, dot, miss 4.

Answer 80
A die.

Answer 81
Albert was a lousy conductor!

Answer 82
There were five men present, but the dealer was a woman.

Answer 83
H (All the letters can be reversed vertically and remain the same).

Answer 84
The men are Siamese twins. The judge wants to know whether they can be separated.

Answer 136

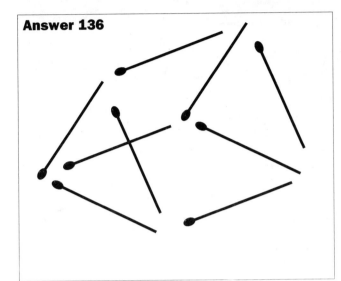

Answer 85
Time.

Answer 86
Over 16,000,000.

Answer 87
Mr White was, or at least his ashes. His last request was that his remains be interred in the local cemetery. The German authorities did not known who to address the urn to and came up with a rather strange solution to their dilemma.

Answer 88
O. The letters represent a number based on their position in the alphabet. The total for each triangle equals 60.

Answer 89
Inwards.

Answer 90
10. The numbers in each row of triangles equal 12, 24, 36, 48, when added together, starting from the top.

Answer 91
Fortunately they reach the bridge at different times.

Answer 92
The man was left-handed. He was injured on a Saturday and went back to work on Monday morning.

Answer 93
Radiating lines = 2; Curved lines = 4; Black = 6.

Answer 94
39. The sum of each adjacent pair of top numbers is halved to get the value underneath.

Answer 95
$5. The men were a grandfather, his son and grandson.

Answer 96
The arteries, veins and capillaries in your own body.

Answer 97
$14 \times 2 \div 7 + 11 - 4 \times 6 = 66$.

Answer 98
Dinosaurs and humans never lived at the same time so cave men were never eaten by dinosaurs.

Answer 129
Make a triangle flat on the table and hold the other matches over it to make a pyramid.

Answer 99

B. The figure moves 90 degrees clockwise each time. When diamond is either north or south, then the circle and square change to shaded and unshaded respectively and the arrowhead becomes a square with a diagonal line.

Answer 100

D. Letters take their value from their order in the alphabet, where A = 1, Z = 26. Each 3 letters are added together to give the value at the end of each set, so Q + L + A = 30, moving in a clockwise direction.

Answer 101

61 times.

Answer 102

There are more of them.

Answer 103

If he takes three socks from the drawer he must have a pair, however, since it is totally dark he will still not know which ones he put on!

Answer 138

Pick up the matchbox by forefinger and thumb and bring the case up to your mouth. Suck gently to make the tray stick to the case and then very carefully turn the whole thing over.

Answer 146

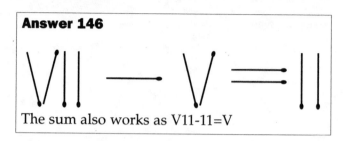

The sum also works as V11-11=V

Answer 104

A. It is the number of spaces beween the crosses.

3	X	1		3	X	1		X	1	2		X	1	2		X	1	2
2	3	4		2	X	1		3	X	1		3	X	1		X	1	2
X	1	2		X	1	2		2	3	4		2	X	1		3	X	1

Answer 105

Flowers = 5; Bubbles = 3; Birds Feet = 1.

Answer 106

K. Position order of the first letter minus that of the second in each section gives the answer next to it e.g. T – N = 6, moving in a clockwise direction.

Answer 107

No, sharks don't sleep.

Answer 108

An hourglass.

Answer 109

B.

Answer 110

5+ ins to the middle.

Answer 111

A square. If the three numbers around the triangle add to an even number the shape is a square; if it is odd, then it is another triangle.

Answer 141

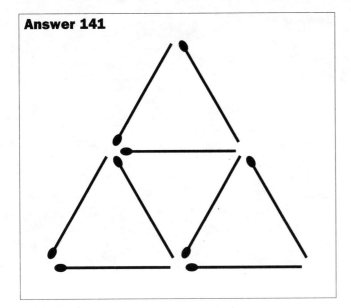

Answer 112
See working on Page 101.

Answer 113
Vertical lines = 2; Blank = 4; Horizontal lines = 6; Zig-zag = 8.

Answer 114
R. Number preceding each pair of letters shows how many letters the second letter is after the first, e.g. P is 5 letters after K in alphabetical order.

Answer 115
F + Q x I + B ÷ K – D = O.

QUICK WIT Answer 116
Zulfiqa Khan was smuggling donkeys.

Answer 117
The mirror actually reverses you back to front.

Answer 118
Because they are two of a set of triplets.

Answer 119
D. Add a cross piece each time, alternating between adding them vertically and horizontally. A vertical cross piece changes the colour of the arrow head.

Answer 120
A.

Answer 121
L – G x F ÷ C + O ÷ E = E.

Answer 122
N. The numbers in each block are added together, then count back from the end of the alphabet that many times to find the letter next to each block (7 2 5 is linked to M and so on). The letter follows the numbers in a clockwise direction.

Answer 123
Press hard on one coin and then use a third coin to strike it smartly on the edge. The force will be transmitted to the coin you mustn't touch which will then skid across the table allowing ample room for the book.

Answer 77

Answer 142

Answer 124

$27 \div 9 \times 6 + 12 \div 3 - 5 = 5$.

Answer 125

The air above the Equator is much colder than the air over the Poles (because at the point there is a greater height of air and therefore the temperature can fall lower).

Answer 126

Although deaf he was not mute, so he shouted 'Shark!'

Answer 127

Fish.

Answer 128

The conductor's baton.

Answer 129

See design on Page 103.

Answer 130

See design on Page 100.

Answer 131

Answer 132

53. The 2 top numbers in each column are added together to give the value underneath.

Answer 133

See design on Page 102.

Answer 134

See design on Page 109.

Answer 135

See design on Page 110.

Answer 136

See design on Page 103.

Answer 137

Push the tray of each box slightly forward and then fit the boxes into each other. This should make quite a strong tower which can be picked up without collapsing.

Answer 138

See design on Page 104.

Answer 145

Answer 139
Put your face directly above the coins and blow very hard into the glass. With a little practice you should be able to get the small coin to jump out onto the table.

Answer 140
See design on Page 112.

Answer 141
See design on Page 105.

Answer 142
See design on Page 106.

Answer 143
See design on Page 101.

Answer 144
See design above right.

Answer 145
See design on Page 106.

Answer 146
See design on Page 104.

Answer 147
See design on Page 109.

Answer 148
Move yourself! If viewed upside down the equation is correct.

Answer 149
See design on right.

Answer 150
See design on Page 108.

Answer 144

Answer 151

X	+	-
X	X	÷
÷	X	+
X	+	-
÷	X	X

Answer 152
156. In each row, the first number multiplied by the third equals the second.

Answer 149

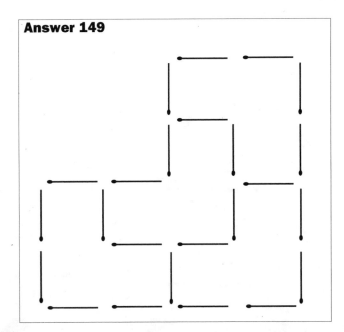

Answer 153
B. The minute hand moves back fifteen minutes and the hour hand moves forward three hours.

Answer 154
D. The second hand moves forward 30 and back 15 seconds alternately, the minute hand moves back 10 and forward five minutes alternately, and the hour hand moves forward two and back one hour alternately.

Answer 155
Dots = 1; Curved lines = 3; Blank = 5; Straight lines = 7.

Answer 156
F is wrong. In all the others the dot is in both the square and the triangle.

Answer 157
Ben Gurion, Gatwick, Las Palmas.

Answer 158
Heathrow, McCoy, O'Hare, Dalaman, Dar Es Salaam, Ho Chi Minh City, Houston, El Paso, Charles De Gaulle, Benito Juarez, Kranebitten.

Answer 159
6. Every small number also has its square value in the circle.

Answer 160
A La Recherche Du Temps Perdu, A Thousand And One Nights, To Kill A Mockingbird.

Answer 161
Edward Albee, Samuel Beckett, Bertholt Brecht, Noel Coward, Anton Chekov, Arthur Miller, Luigi Pirandello, Jean Racine, Sophocles, Tennessee Williams.

Answer 162
Sibling. All the others refer to a specific sex.

Answer 163
Your ship is a space ship and the sea is one of the seas of the moon.

Answer 164
He folded his arms, picked up the ends of the string, unfolded the arms and, hey presto, a knot!

Answer 165
See design on Page 115.

Answer 166
See design on Page 116.

Answer 167
See design on Page 114.

Answer 168
Jodie Foster, Marlon Brando, Cybill Shepherd, Claudia Cardinale, Roman Polanski, Daniel Day Lewis, Robert Redford, Walter Matthau, Woody Allen, Dudley Moore.

Answer 169
Because a round cover cannot fall back down a hole.

Answer 150

Answer 147

Answer 170

Augustus, Caligula, Claudius, Diocletian, Galba, Nero, Tiberius, Trajan, Valerian, Vespasian.

Answer 179

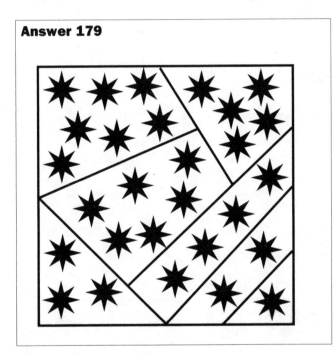

Answer 171

Bobby Ford in the Bronx isn't married to Donna, Anna, Betsy, or Joan, so he must be married to Mary whose former husband was Dick Jones. Mary didn't come from the Bronx, Queens, Staten Island or Manhattan, so she must have come from Brooklyn. Bobby didn't come from the Bronx or Brooklyn, Queens or Manhattan, so he must have come from Staten Island, which means his former wife was Betsy. Joan Martin's former husband was wasn't Bobby or Dick, Hank or Dave (her present husband), so he must be Jim Lewis from Manhattan. She and Dave can't live in the Bronx or Manhattan, Brooklyn or Staten Island, so they must live in Queens. Dave didn't come from Brooklyn, Staten Island,

Manhattan or Queens, so he must have come from the Bronx. His former wife wasn't Mary, Anna or Betsy, so she must have been Donna. Dick Jones married to Betsy, came from Brooklyn. He doesn't live in the Bronx, Brooklyn, Queens or Staten Island, so he must live in Manhattan. Jim Lewis from Manhattan Joan's former husband), is married to Anna Smith from Queens and lives in Brooklyn. Therefore Hank Smith married Donna from the Bronx and they live in Staten Island.

	Ex-Wife	Ex-Home	New Wife	New Home
Bobby Ford	Betsy	Staten I.	Mary	Bronx
Dick Jones	Mary	Brooklyn	Betsy	M'hattan
Jim Lewis	Joan	M'hattan	Anna	Brooklyn
Dave Martin	Donna	Bronx	Joan	Queens
Hank Smith	Anna	Queens	Donna	Staten I.

Answer 172

1st: John (68 min, 22 sec)
2nd: Ivan (68 min, 27 sec)
3rd: Bruce (68 min, 35 sec)
4th: Pedro (68 min, 40 sec)
5th: Pierre (68 min, 53 sec).

Answer 134

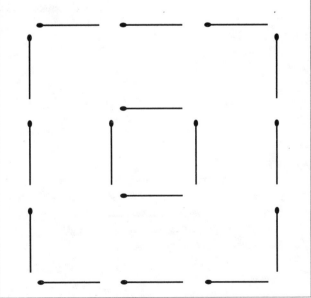

Answer 135
The square root of 1 is 1.

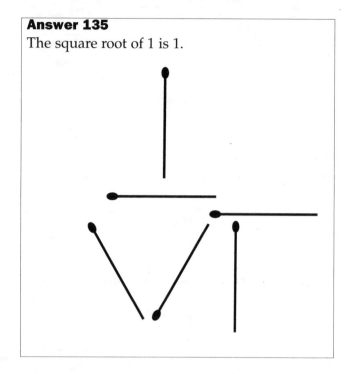

Answer 173

72	÷	9	x	5	=	40
–		–		+		÷
18	+	6	–	4	=	20
54	÷	3	÷	9	=	2

Answer 174
Piece C. The pattern is 3 hearts, 3 diamonds, 3 spades; 2 hearts, 2 diamonds, 2 spades; 1 heart, 1 diamond and 1 spade repeated. It starts at the top left corner and moves back and forth across the grid in a bustrophedon pattern.

Answer 175
Piece B. The sequence is 3 stars, 2 triangles, 1 cross; 1 star, 2 triangles, 3 crosses; 3 stars, 3 triangles, 3 crosses repeated. The pattern starts at the bottom left and repeats in a vertical bustrophedon.

Answer 176
Piece A. The pattern is 2 circles, 2 squares, 2 triangles; 3 circles, 2 squares, 3 triangles; 1 circle, 2 squares, 1 triangle repeated. The pattern starts at the top right and goes round the grid clockwise in an inward spiral.

Answer 177
As Neville has a drive five times longer than that of Pauline, and they drive for 60 minutes between them, Neville must have a 50-minute journey in the sports car and Pauline a 10-minute drive. Lynda's drive is five times the length of Martin's so she must have a 25-minute journey, while Martin has a 5-minute drive in his estate car, because it is half of Pauline's journey time. Therefore, Olivia has a 40-minute drive in the saloon, Pauline is in the van and Lynda drives the convertible.

Lynda	25 minutes	convertible
Martin	5 minutes	estate
Neville	50 minutes	sports
Olivia	40 minutes	saloon
Pauline	10 minutes	van

Answer 178

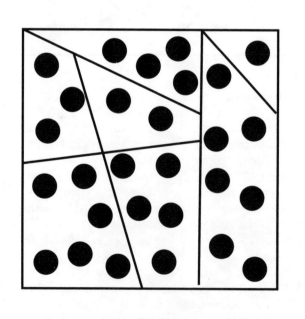

Answer 178
See design on Page 110.

Answer 179
See design on Page 109.

Answer 180
Dustin Hoffman   Derek Jacobi
Paul Newman   Julia Roberts
Arnold Schwarzenegger
Anjelica Huston   Demi Moore
Nastassja Kinski   Winona Ryder

Answer 181
B. There is no triangle intersection on the odd one.

Answer 182
D. The shape is laterally transposed and then reflected down the dividing line.

Answer 183
C.

Answer 184
B. The sequence here is less one dot, plus two dots, and the box rotates in a clockwise direction for each dot.

Answer 185
D. All except D have odd number of edges.

Answer 186
We are talking about a chess game.

Answer 187
D. Circle and triangle alternate. After a circle the next figure moves round one space, staying on the same side of the line. After a triangle it moves on 2.

Answer 188
E. Left half reflected to form symmetrical shape, then half of right half is reflected back.

Answer 189
A.

Answer 190
C. The smallest segment is rotated 90 degrees clockwise. The middle segment remains static. Largest segment rotated 90 degrees anti or counter clockwise.

Answer 191
B.

Answer 192
E. Largest shape is reflected horizontally and the size order is reversed.

Answer 193
B. In all other cases the smaller circle is within the larger circle.

Answer 194
E. A dotted V shape is added each time with dots alternating between being at the start and at the end of each V added. The leading edge of a new V overlaps the undotted edge of the previous V.

Answer 195
Andy's mother and aunt were identical twins.

Answer 196
D. An unshaded ringed planet becomes a shaded ringed planet; a star containing a shaded planet becomes an unshaded planet; a shaded ringed planet becomes an unshaded ringed planet; an unshaded planet becomes a star containing a shaded planet. The symbols are then vertically reflected.

Answer 197
They are sisters.

Answer 198
You don't bury survivors.

Answer 199
Only one – after that it isn't empty any more.

Answer 200
B.

Answer 201
E. Rotate one place clockwise and then reflect across a horizontal line through the middle of the figure.

Answer 202
D. Top row of letters go back in alphabetical order 3 places each time. The middle row goes forward 2, 3, 4, 5 places. Bottom row goes back 8, 4, 2, 1 places.

Answer 203
Yes. And a 5th, 6th, 7th...

Answer 204
9. Each vowel is worth 4. Each consonant is worth 3. The sum of each set of letters gives the total following each set, in a clockwise direction.

Answer 205
A. A single line can be added to make three, not upside down, capital letters. The others already have 3.

Answer 206
He decided to go for a binge on the way home, got talking, and didn't arrive home until 6.43 the following morning.

Answer 207
C. Curved lines gradually encroach on space within triangle.

Answer 208
D. One tip of the star is missing.

Answer 209
D. Add 2 lines, then 1, 2, 1. Rotate slightly each time.

Answer 210
C. Small square becomes a big square and vice versa. A small square with a triangle goes to small square alone. A triangle on big square remains a triangle.

Answer 140

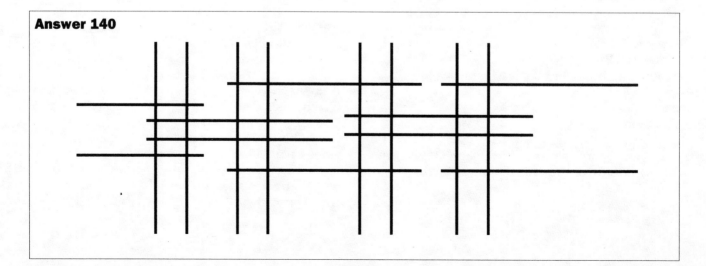

Answer 211
Only 30 minutes. The alarm clock went off at 9.00 pm.

Answer 212
D. One end of the rectangle should fit inside the circle. The arrow should cut through the rectangle in such a way as to make 2 four sided shapes. The arrow must be outside the circle.

Answer 213
A. In the other cases the addition of a vertical or horizontal straight line would form a capital letter.

Answer 214
He was talking about his heart.

Answer 215
A. The inner shape becomes outer shape, the shape surrounding it fits inside, then shape at top. The remainder is then shrunk and put inside the middle shape. A shaded shape covers an unshaded shape.

Answer 216
C. It is the only instance where a square is not touching a triangle.

Answer 217
D. The diagonal line sloping up from left to right becomes horizontal. Vertical lines stay vertical. Diagonal lines sloping down from left to right slope up. Where a square contains a triangle the whole square is flipped vertically.

Answer 218
They were buying digits for their house number. Four at $3 each cost $12.

Answer 219
A circle in the second triangle on the bottom row. Starting from the top, working from left to right, sequence of square, miss 2 , triangle, circle, miss 1, square, miss 2, and so on.

Answer 220
False teeth.

Answer 221
He shaves.

Answer 222
C, the rectangle. A shape with an odd number of edges is followed by one with an even number, working down from left to right.

Answer 223
C.

Answer 224
D. If you add together the total number of sides of all the shapes, D is the only one with an odd total.

Answer 225
A. The middle shape becomes the outside shape. A shaded shape covers an unshaded shape.

Answer 226
B. In all other cases there are two white and two black triangles at the corners.

Answer 227
B. The number of straight lines doubles each time

Answer 228
32. Working along each row from left to right, (A + B) x C − D = E.

Answer 229
F. The number 8 is the only one which is symmetrical.

Answer 167

G	A	C	H	I	N	A	T	O	W	N	U	L	H	V	R	E	G	S	O
Z	R	B	L	T	N	O	S	I	D	A	M	I	Y	X	N	N	O	I	P
R	T	E	U	A	C	S	B	L	D	F	G	T	H	R	T	R	K	M	E
A	L	G	E	P	R	Q	Q	S	A	C	T	T	A	V	Z	Y	X	A	H
R	I	B	Q	N	Z	N	O	U	P	R	C	L	A	C	B	A	L	A	A
S	N	K	A	C	W	R	A	M	A	B	R	E	I	T	A	L	Y	I	L
D	C	G	E	L	E	I	O	N	D	R	O	N	N	O	T	T	I	L	N
G	O	H	A	T	M	N	C	E	W	C	E	T	A	H	S	T	L	U	E
S	L	W	N	A	V	E	S	H	E	Y	G	I	T	H	A	I	S	N	I
S	N	E	A	P	A	I	V	M	N	A	I	M	N	T	H	R	E	H	A
R	C	S	E	G	E	I	I	T	R	T	I	E	S	G	M	O	L	Q	N
C	I	T	Y	E	L	E	Y	O	D	E	N	S	Q	U	A	R	E	E	U
L	L	A	H	L	H	T	O	F	L	A	Y	T	A	D	I	U	M	R	M
L	T	O	A	N	B	R	O	N	X	C	S	P	A	R	K	N	I	S	L
I	K	G	E	E	G	E	T	T	R	I	E	E	K	N	A	Y	N	G	B
L	E	S	O	G	O	D	F	E	R	O	M	L	A	S	T	R	O	O	N
E	I	T	O	G	A	T	M	E	W	R	F	I	A	T	I	I	N	N	G
T	H	H	E	U	S	A	E	B	L	O	I	N	G	T	P	U	Z	B	Z
L	O	E	S	G	R	A	L	D	T	H	E	G	N	I	D	L	I	U	T
T	I	M	E	G	I	T	B	R	O	O	K	L	Y	N	I	S	A	P	A

114

Answer 165

M	I	F	T	E	P	Z	L	E	I	R	U	E	P	D	T	M	E	R	B
A	A	D	I	H	U	Z	N	E	S	H	A	L	E	R	O	H	N	E	O
N	G	D	H	T	E	I	E	M	S	A	A	E	R	M	S	U	E	M	I
C	H	H	E	S	E	Y	O	E	S	F	G	S	E	U	T	B	L	U	S
A	R	D	E	L	L	I	W	N	A	F	A	O	L	E	I	I	L	T	D
G	A	R	D	E	O	N	D	E	I	Y	Y	N	A	W	N	L	L	R	E
Y	T	R	E	O	A	M	T	H	M	R	E	I	C	L	H	R	A	S	B
O	D	E	C	H	D	E	P	E	O	W	T	L	H	T	E	Y	O	S	O
U	T	H	C	T	Y	A	R	S	P	S	T	E	A	F	R	A	N	U	U
M	E	A	T	H	E	C	O	M	E	O	E	D	I	O	D	E	G	O	L
M	J	A	R	D	I	N	D	O	U	L	E	G	S	S	A	C	R	E	O
C	H	C	T	P	R	E	E	R	N	H	Y	R	E	R	U	E	O	C	G
A	R	A	E	R	S	A	S	A	D	T	I	S	D	J	U	I	K	H	N
T	C	A	R	S	A	D	P	F	N	I	S	E	I	S	T	L	E	T	E
C	T	O	H	C	I	S	L	E	L	I	B	E	R	T	E	L	I	L	E
L	E	P	R	E	D	D	A	N	T	E	S	S	E	A	Y	L	T	T	S
I	Y	E	S	T	E	G	M	T	M	O	N	T	M	A	R	T	R	E	O
C	T	R	E	T	Y	R	U	E	D	E	R	I	V	O	L	I	D	O	N
H	H	A	R	W	A	T	H	E	Y	A	B	E	E	N	E	T	U	O	R
Y	N	D	I	O	M	P	H	E	H	V	E	L	O	U	V	R	E	E	A

Answer 166

```
A N O W T H W E S T M I N S T E R E K R
B C L A Q P O D Y U P D P Z Z L E F I I
N I H T S I H E S T I Y U U A R E D N W
H A E E C N A R E T L H C E Q S E P G E
O P R R L C E G O L I N G I T S O C S O
U I G L O O A H I U W P S R O M R E C C
A S N H T H A D T S H W H C U S A A R T
I G C W A S O H O N I T T O K O H G O E
R E I R S I M L J G T I N G N W L M S Y
G U T O O T N E D G E H A L L A U N S T
A N S D W S S H R T A T D O F B O G K I
G O L D E N E T A O F O R A M D Y N T R
O L E B S O U K G W E Y R U N C K A I L
U B A Q S L R T T E L T F O A P L G H T
E I U F Y A O N U R O F L L A M C A N S
R A R O P A E E T H S T A Y A U E A B Y
E A D E L V R L G I N C S H O R L R L A
R A D M O R A L E E E C G P A R I E T Y
E Y S C A T B U C K I N W H A D Y N O U
H N O T C H E L S E A J O E G R K Z O O
```

The desire to understand the inner workings of the human mind is an ancient one. Human beings are social animals and whether they are operating together or in competition, it is vital to understand what other members of their social group might be thinking and how they are likely to react. Furthermore, we are naturally inquisitive creatures and have a fascination with ourselves.

Psychometrics, the science of mental measurement, has made enormous strides since its discovery at the end of the last century. However, because psychometric tests have to be administered by trained individuals, they are not usually available to the public. Does this mean that we are to be denied the fun of self-discovery? Certainly not. The tests in this book are designed with just that purpose... and used with common sense they should prove very revealing. If you want to enlarge on a particular aspect of your personality profile, Mensa offers scientific psychometric assessments run by trained personnel. To contact Mensa, see the address provided on pages 6-7.

YOU AND YOUR
CAREER

Choosing or changing your career is one of the most important decisions you ever make. Getting it wrong may have serious consequences for your future happiness. Yet few people give enough thought to their career choice even though it is one they will have to live with for a long time. So use the tests in this section to assess your career potential. The questions will not only help you to identify strengths and weaknesses, but also help to crystallize what you want out of life and how to get it.

LIFEPLAN

Most people drift through life and just let things happen to them. They get up, go to work, come home and never question whether they really enjoy their job or whether they might be more fulfilled in another line of work. This questionnaire gives you the opportunity to set down what you want out of your work and give yourself ideas on how to achieve your aims. There are absolutely no right or wrong answers. There are not even any scores. If you feel that any part of the questionnaire does not apply to you, just leave it out.

SECTION 1: THE OFFICE

Do you work in an office/factory/hospital? Do you really like it? Do you work a conventional 9-5 day in an office? Would you prefer another option such as tele-working or job-sharing? These questions might help to clarify the issue for you.

YES   NO

1. Do you like the camaraderie of office life? ☐ ☐
2. Do you mind working fixed hours? ☐ ☐
3. Does your office have flexitime and, if not, would you like it? ☐ ☐
4. Does your office insist on a code of dress? ☐ ☐
5. Would you rather be able to wear what you wanted? ☐ ☐
6. Do you socialize with your workmates? ☐ ☐
7. Do you dislike office politics? ☐ ☐
8. Do you form friendly or sexual relationships at work? ☐ ☐
9. Is there much back-biting in your workplace? ☐ ☐
10. Could you work on your own, for example, at home? ☐ ☐
11. If you worked at home, would you feel lonely and cut off? ☐ ☐
12. Would you actually like to get away from office life? ☐ ☐
13. Would you prefer to job-share rather than work full time? ☐ ☐
14. If you worked for a company from your own home, would you feel left out of things? ☐ ☐
15. Instead of working at home, would you like to work in a tele-cottage? ☐ ☐

SECTION 2: MOTIVATION

People have different reasons for their career choice. Some might find that income is their deciding factor but for others it might be job satisfaction. These questions should help you understand what motivates you.

		YES	NO
1	Working at home would allow you to see more of your family. Do you actually want to see more of them?	☐	☐
2	Would you prefer to work your own hours - for example, take the afternoon off and work all evening?	☐	☐
3	Would you consider doing a less well-paid job if it gave more satisfaction?	☐	☐
4	Would you like the opportunity to earn more even though you might have to spend more time at the office?	☐	☐
5	Do you enjoy the feeling of a job well done?	☐	☐
6	Do you consider your work of benefit to the community?	☐	☐
7	Do you feel that your work achieves anything of lasting value?	☐	☐
8	Do you enjoy a position of power in your organization?	☐	☐
9	Is it important to you to attain a position of authority?	☐	☐
10	Are you satisfied being "just a cog in the wheel" of your organization?	☐	☐
11	Would you like to be your own boss?	☐	☐
12	Does your job make full use of your abilities?	☐	☐
13	Does your work require an element of creativity?	☐	☐
14	Do you thrive in a tense, stressful environment?	☐	☐
15	Do you resent taking orders?	☐	☐
16	Does an element of risk add spice to your life?	☐	☐
17	Would you risk being self-employed?	☐	☐

		YES	NO
18	Is promotion an important part of your career plan?	☐	☐
19	Would you be willing to devote a lifetime to your current job?	☐	☐
20	Do you thrive on the hustle and bustle of city environments?	☐	☐
21	Do you find the rules and regulations of company life irksome?	☐	☐
22	Would you do a job you dislike if it was very well paid?	☐	☐
23	Do you have enough self-discipline to follow your own work schedule without being told what to do?	☐	☐
24	Do you feel the need for a complete change of direction?	☐	☐
25	Would you like to have chosen another career?	☐	☐
26	Would you like to work for a large company?	☐	☐
27	Would you do an unpopular job (traffic warden, tax inspector)?	☐	☐
28	Would you like to work in a fiercely competitive environment?	☐	☐
29	Would you consider a job where you are highly valued by the community but poorly paid?	☐	☐
30	Would you risk your savings, home, etc, on an entrepreneurial venture?	☐	☐
31	Is job security a high priority for you?	☐	☐
32	Would you take an insecure job that was very well paid?	☐	☐
33	Would you consider a job that had an element of personal danger, such as one in the emergency services?	☐	☐
34	Do you get the training you need to advance your career?	☐	☐
35	Do you think of your colleagues as friends?	☐	☐

		YES	NO

SECTION 3: ENTHUSIASM

		YES	NO
1	Do you look forward to going to work each day?	☐	☐
2	Do you like working in town?	☐	☐
3	Is your job so demanding that it destroys your social life?	☐	☐
4	Is your job so demanding it adversely affects family relationships?	☐	☐
5	Do you like your job but hate the place you work in?	☐	☐
6	Did you choose your job or just drift into it?	☐	☐
7	Do you regret your choice of job?	☐	☐
8	Is it too late to change to your dream career?	☐	☐
9	Would you like outdoor work?	☐	☐
10	Would you like to meet a lot of people during the course of your work?	☐	☐
11	Would you feel more comfortable working for a small concern like a family business?	☐	☐
12	Would you feel more secure in a government job such as the armed forces or civil service?	☐	☐
13	Would you take an insecure job that was very well paid?	☐	☐
14	Would you be happier working mainly with members of your own sex?	☐	☐
15	Would you consider working in partnership with your spouse or children?	☐	☐
16	Would you like to own a family firm you could leave to your children?	☐	☐

SECTION 4: LOGISTICS

		YES	NO
1	Do you have to travel far to work and, if so, do you mind?	☐	☐
2	Working at home would cut out travel. Is this an attractive proposition?	☐	☐
3	Do you prefer to travel around rather than work in one place?	☐	☐
4	Would you mind a job where you frequently had to move house?	☐	☐
5	Would you like to work abroad?	☐	☐

		YES	**NO**

SECTION 5: YOUR PERFORMANCE

1 Do you have problems at work? If so, what are they? ☐ ☐

2 Do you find that in each job you take the same problems occur? ☐ ☐

3 Do you think that your work is satisfactory? ☐ ☐

4 Do your employers find you a good worker? ☐ ☐

5 If you have been seriously criticized for your performance, was such criticism justified? ☐ ☐

6 Do you feel you have been unfairly held back on grounds of race, sex, etc? ☐ ☐

7 Do you feel you have achieved all that you could have done? ☐ ☐

8 Are you, on the whole, satisfied with your career so far? ☐ ☐

9 Has your career followed the course you thought it would? ☐ ☐

10 Do you feel you cannot get any further in your current job? ☐ ☐

11 Do you feel you have been unfairly passed over for promotion? ☐ ☐

12 Would you like a job where you are constantly judged on your performance? ☐ ☐

SECTION 6: EARNINGS, QUALIFICATIONS AND ASPIRATIONS

1 Make a careful estimate of what you earn. Include things like company pension plans, a company car and any other benefits. Also make allowances for incidental benefits (for example, if you work so close to where you live that you do not have to pay for childcare, then estimate how much that saves you).

_____ £ / $ _____ . _____

_____ £ / $ _____ . _____

_____ £ / $ _____ . _____

_____ £ / $ _____ . _____

2   Write out a careful list of ALL your qualifications and skills.
Include everything from PhDs to first aid certificates.
Summarize absolutely everything you have to offer.

	Grade
_____	Grade .
_____	Grade .
_____	Grade .
_____	Grade .
_____	Grade .
_____	Grade .
_____	Grade .
_____	Grade .
_____	Grade .

3   Would you like to gain further qualifications?
List those which you could go after.

_____

_____

_____

_____

4   Do you feel you have insufficient education and training to make
progress in your career?

In career terms, where do you hope to be in

a) Five years' time?
_____

b) Ten years' time?
_____

CAREER OR VOCATION?

This questionnaire looks at your interests, preferences and feelings about a variety of things. It will examine a number of facets of your personality which are important in your career. The results should enable you to judge whether you are in the right job and, if not, what sort of career would suit you better. There is no time limit. There are no right or wrong answers. Remember that all career choices will also be linked to intellectual ability. You must take into account your performance on the aptitude tests when you consider what work you would like to do. Be as honest in your responses as you can - only you will ever see them. Answer all the questions.

		YES	NO
1	I am a very logical rational person.	☐	☐
2	People are always asking me to help with practical tasks.	☐	☐
3	I would examine a set of accounts to discover a small error even if it took all day.	☐	☐
4	I like tinkering with cars.	☐	☐
5	At school I preferred art and literature to chemistry and physics.	☐	☐
6	I am good at coping with crises.	☐	☐
7	Being a leader is tiresome and difficult.	☐	☐
8	I was always good at science at school.	☐	☐
9	The life of a school teacher would suit me.	☐	☐
10	I have never done anything dangerous just for fun.	☐	☐
11	If you want things done properly, you must do them yourself.	☐	☐

QUESTIONNAIRES

		YES	NO
12	I have always been good at maths.	☐	☐
13	I am quite quiet and reserved.	☐	☐
14	Office systems and procedures bore me to tears.	☐	☐
15	I never mind speaking in public.	☐	☐
16	Music is an important part of my life.	☐	☐
17	I normally feel able to cope with life.	☐	☐
18	The problems of artificial intelligence fascinate me.	☐	☐
19	Managing staff would be a pain in the neck.	☐	☐
20	I have always been mechanically minded.	☐	☐
21	I like computer games.	☐	☐
22	I can't understand what makes people want to gamble.	☐	☐
23	It must be fun being an actor.	☐	☐
24	People ask me to take charge because I am good at what I do.	☐	☐
25	Variety is the spice of life.	☐	☐
26	A career in sales would excite me.	☐	☐
27	I have read books which changed my life.	☐	☐
28	Helping problem families would be an interesting and useful thing to do.	☐	☐
29	I like to be in charge.	☐	☐
30	Computer games distract children from more useful pastimes.	☐	☐
31	I hate being on my own.	☐	☐
32	Noise often distracts me from the task in hand.	☐	☐
33	I like anything involving figures.	☐	☐
34	Government sponsorship of the arts is a waste of money.	☐	☐

		YES	NO

35 I would prefer to look at a great car than a great painting. ☐ ☐

36 I would like to explore far-off places. ☐ ☐

37 Every day should present a different challenge. ☐ ☐

38 I dislike crowds. ☐ ☐

39 Filing and clerical work may not be glamorous, but they have to be done and I am good at them. ☐ ☐

40 I feel depressed without people around me. ☐ ☐

41 I take a great interest in other people's problems. ☐ ☐

42 Music can move me deeply. ☐ ☐

43 I often feel vaguely unwell for no good reason. ☐ ☐

44 I don't like being told what to do. ☐ ☐

45 I hate routine tasks. ☐ ☐

46 A visit to a nuclear power station would make an interesting day out. ☐ ☐

47 I enjoy trying to make people accept my views. ☐ ☐

48 Caring for the mentally handicapped would be too distressing. ☐ ☐

49 I like to be surrounded by people. ☐ ☐

50 A little danger adds spice to life. ☐ ☐

51 I should like to live for some months in a space laboratory. ☐ ☐

52 I have often wanted to write a novel. ☐ ☐

53 I am a natural leader. ☐ ☐

54 It irritates me when people bungle simple tasks like putting in a screw. ☐ ☐

55 I could not work in an office all day. ☐ ☐

56 Machines are more reliable than people. ☐ ☐

		YES	NO
57	People regard me as level-headed and capable.	☐	☐
58	I dislike criticism from others.	☐	☐
59	I would rather get on with a practical task than waste time writing or painting.	☐	☐
60	I find changes in my routine unsettling.	☐	☐
61	I would enjoy the job of a research scientist.	☐	☐
62	I can usually persuade people to my point of view.	☐	☐
63	I get pleasure from making things.	☐	☐
64	A career in advertising would suit me.	☐	☐
65	I would be attracted to a job which involves a lot of travel.	☐	☐
66	I dislike parties where I don't know anyone.	☐	☐
67	I would rather let others take responsibility.	☐	☐
68	Computers are too complicated for me to understand.	☐	☐
69	The life of a travelling salesperson appeals to me.	☐	☐
70	I understand which laws of physics govern the working of an engine.	☐	☐
71	I often suffer from an upset stomach for no reason.	☐	☐
72	I enjoy designing systems to make things more efficient.	☐	☐
73	I tend to organize people.	☐	☐
74	I would much rather people did not bring their problems to me.	☐	☐
75	I am attracted to thrilling sports such as skiing or hang-gliding.	☐	☐
76	I should like to be a contestant on a TV game show.	☐	☐
77	Science will enable humanity to achieve feats our grandparents could not have dreamt of.	☐	☐
78	I find computers fascinating.	☐	☐

		YES	NO
79	I have a good eye for detail.	☐	☐
80	Most people would describe me as the life and soul of the party.	☐	☐
81	I would enjoy the life of an artist.	☐	☐
82	I would rather take a job which promised substantial but uncertain rewards than work steadily for a fixed salary.	☐	☐
83	I prefer to get on with a job on my own.	☐	☐
84	I really enjoy understanding how machines work.	☐	☐
85	I like to be with people.	☐	☐
86	I can understand the fascination of gambling.	☐	☐
87	People who waste time on the arts never achieve anything.	☐	☐
88	I like the security of a set routine.	☐	☐
89	I find it very hard to work in messy surroundings.	☐	☐
90	Practical people are more valuable to society than academics.	☐	☐
91	Looking after disabled children would interest me.	☐	☐
92	I enjoy solving puzzles and crosswords.	☐	☐
93	I find I am able to cope in most circumstances.	☐	☐
94	Social events are more fun if you go in a crowd.	☐	☐
95	I like to know what I will be doing each day.	☐	☐
96	It is important for someone to cross the Ts and dot the Is.	☐	☐
97	I can usually get my own way in the end.	☐	☐
98	The work of a nurse would be rewarding.	☐	☐
99	I have often been asked to speak in public.	☐	☐
100	It annoys me that some people can't change a light bulb for themselves.	☐	☐
101	People should sort out their own lives.	☐	☐

		YES	NO
102	Logic problems present an interesting challenge.	☐	☐
103	Being a police officer would be a good way of helping the community.	☐	☐
104	I can talk persuasively on almost any topic.	☐	☐
105	It gives me great satisfaction to mend things.	☐	☐
106	People who fuss about the adverse effects of scientific research fail to understand its great importance.	☐	☐
107	Social workers should spend less time meddling in other people's affairs.	☐	☐
108	I would enjoy training as an accountant.	☐	☐
109	I would like to be a politician.	☐	☐
110	I sometimes lose my temper for no good reason.	☐	☐
111	I could never work in a boring job just because the money was good.	☐	☐
112	I hate problems involving maths.	☐	☐
113	Science has made a greater contribution to human progress than all of the arts put together.	☐	☐
114	Clerical work is boring and trivial.	☐	☐
115	I get fits of depression for no real reason.	☐	☐
116	I would find bookkeeping an interesting career.	☐	☐
117	I find it easy to contribute to meetings and group discussions.	☐	☐
118	Being a clerical assistant would be too boring for me.	☐	☐
119	I would be interested in studying viruses under a microscope.	☐	☐
120	I would enjoy freelance work which involved constant changes and new challenges.	☐	☐

APTITUDE TEST A

NUMERICAL ABILITY

Nowadays when you go after a new job you are likely to be given aptitude tests which measure real-world skills such as numerical and verbal ability. The knack to these tests is to work as quickly as you possibly can. Do all the questions which seem easy and come back to the harder ones later. You will probably feel that too little time has been allowed to complete the test. This is a deliberate tactic on the part of the test-setters and is intended to prevent too many people from getting all the answers right. If this happened, the test would fail to differentiate between the best candidates and there would be what is known as a "ceiling effect".

TIME LIMIT: 30 MINS.

1   What number comes next in the series: 2, 3, 5, 9?   _____

2   If a family wastes a quarter of each pint of milk they buy, how much milk will they consume after purchasing 12 pints?   _____

3   If A = 13, B = 3A - 7, and C = 2B + 5, what does that make 4C equal?   _____

4   Assuming a motorbike is moving at a constant speed, if it takes 4 hours and 20 minutes to cover 260 miles, how many miles are covered each hour?   _____

5   If B + A = 7 and A - B = 3, what are the numerical values of A and B?   _____

6   What number is half the value of 5 multiplied by the square root of 64?   _____

7 If 3 eggs are required to make an omelette, and 10% of 5 dozen eggs are bad, how many omelettes can be made from this batch?

_____

8 How many parasites will exist after 4 days if every parasite splits into 2 each day, and a population of 7 exists on day 1?

_____

9 If a quarter of the number of people in an office each have a cup of tea, a sixth have water, half have coffee, and the remaining two have nothing, how many people are there altogether?

_____

10 When a bus travels at 38 mph for 30 minutes, then at 8 mph during rush hour for 15 minutes, then joins a main road and travels at 60 mph for 1 hour and 5 minutes, what is the total distance covered?

_____

11 What number comes next in the series: 2, 4, 16?

_____

12 A primary school has an enrolment of 140 pupils. If 15% are vegetarians and 5% are orthodox Jews, how many children can eat the pork stew served for lunch?

_____

13 The volume of a box with sides of length P, Q and R equals P x Q x R. If P = 20, Q = 15 and the volume equals 9,000, what does R equal?

_____

14 What number is as much bigger than 3 x 3 as it is smaller than 5 x 5?

_____

15 How much money will a shareholder earn in total if she sells 500 shares at 3 units each, initially costing 2.45 units, and 350 shares at 3.1 units each, initially costing 3.2 units?

_____

16 If a boy eats 6 peppermints every day, how many weeks will it take him to devour a bumper box of 210?

_____

17 A lump sum of 1,000 units is invested in a savings account. After how many complete years will the investment reach 1,450 units if 10% interest is earned each year?

_____

18 What number comes next in the series: 4, 10, 22, 46?

_____

19 What do P and Q equal if P + Q = 15, P x Q = 54, and P - Q = 3?

_____

20 If a cassette has 90 minutes of playing time, how many cassettes will be needed to record 4 compact discs with playing times of 91, 97, 88 and 102 minutes, and how much blank tape will be left over?

_____

21 When a man jogs at a speed of 5 mph, how long will it take him to cover a distance of 13 miles?

_____

22 A clock reads 2:00 on Monday afternoon. If it is running slow, and losing 3 minutes every two hours, what time will the clock show when it is actually 8:00 on Tuesday evening? _____

23 Some square bathroom tiles each consist of a pattern of 3 triangles fitted together. When a wall is covered with 135 such triangles, how many tiles have been used? _____

24 Each child at a party is given 2 balloons, a piece of cake, and 3 jelly beans. 27 children attend, 5 of whom do not want jelly beans. How many items will be given altogether? _____

25 What number comes next in the series: 360, 72, 18, 6? _____

26 What number comes next in the series: 250, 50, 10? _____

27 Three builders working together each lay 96 bricks an hour. How many hours would it take them to build a wall consisting of 7,200 bricks? _____

28 Marigold seeds can be bought in packets of 32. If 75% of the seeds, when planted properly, are expected to flower, how many marigolds will bloom when six packets of seeds are planted? _____

29 Orange juice is delivered every day to a hotel. If 9 cartons are delivered on Monday, 13 on Tuesday, 21 on Wednesday and 37 on Thursday, how many cartons would you expect to be delivered on Sunday? _____

30 What do A and B equal if 2A + 3B = 29 and 5B - 5 = 30? _____

31 When S is 20% of the value of T, which is a third of the value of U, which is 4 and a half times the value of V, which equals 24, what does S equal? _____

32 A child shares out her marbles so that each of her friends are given the number of marbles equal to 2 times their ages in years. How many marbles are needed for a group of seven 8 year olds, three 9 year olds, and five 10 year olds? _____

33 What number comes next in the series : 4, 10, 25? _____

34 Following a rainstorm, the level of water in a barrel has risen from 13mm to 37mm. If the water level rose at a constant rate of 3mm every 2 minutes, for how long did the rainstorm last? _____

35 What number is as much more than 2 dozen as 2 is less than half a dozen? _____

36 What does X equal when 7X - 12 = 5X + 6? _____

37 An appliance is used 56 times before breaking down. If it has been used 3 times every other day during a certain period, how many complete weeks will it have worked, counting from the first day it is used? _____

38 When Tom is 7 his mother is 4 times as old as him. Her father is, at the same time, twice as old as her. How old was Tom's grandfather when Tom was born? _____

39 A cat has 2 litters of 5 kittens, 40% of whom each eventually have 3 litters of 2 kittens, the remainder each having 2 litters of 4. How many cats are there altogether, assuming none have died? _____

40 If a necklace is made by using 17 red, 39 orange and 136 black beads, how many orange and black beads are needed to complete the necklace for which 340 red beads have already been used? _____

41 If each letter of the alphabet is worth 3 times its order value, with A as number 1 and Z as number 26, what is the total value of all the letters in the alphabet? _____

42 What number comes next in the series: 8, 12, 18, 26? _____

43 A game consists of counters, each labelled with 1 letter of the alphabet. Each of the 5 vowels features on 4 counters, while each consonant features on 3. How many counters are there altogether? _____

44 What do Y and Z equal when 5X = 30, and 7X = 21Y = 14Z? _____

45 What letter is as many letters more than F as S is less than X? _____

46 Twenty-two percent of a batch of 50 batteries last approximately 8 hours, 36% last 9.5 hours, and the remainder last about 11. For how many hours will all of the batteries have worked in total? _____

47 Eight out of every 10 people surveyed claimed to have never committed a crime. Assuming none were lying, how many people out of the sample of 570 have committed a crime? _____

48 A cube is made up of 6 sides, so how many cubes will 138 sides make up? _____

49 What does A equal if B + C = 12, 15 - C = 8, and A x B x C = 105? _____

APTITUDE TEST B

VERBAL ABILITY

Being able to handle a large vocabulary is one fairly reliable indicator of intelligence. There are, of course, exceptions (such as people who experience reading difficulties), but most people of above average intelligence will have a considerable stock of words at their command. See how you get on with these. The test involves having to decide what the target word means and then choose the word whose meaning is closest to it. The words start off quite simple and get progressively harder.

TIME LIMIT: 10 MINUTES.

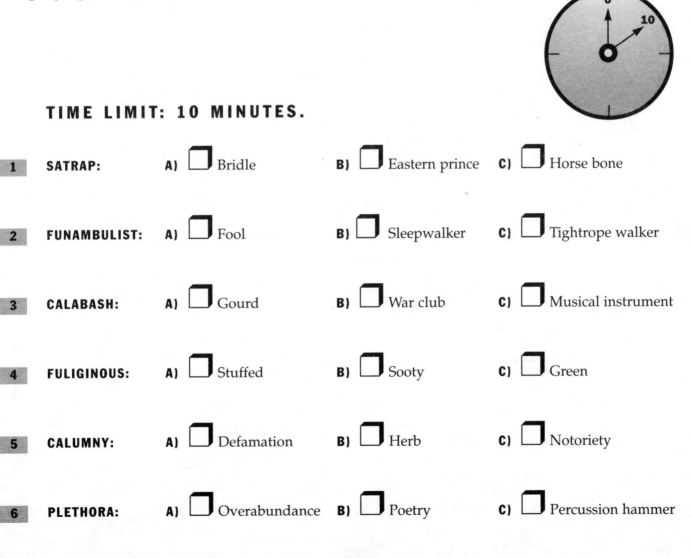

1	SATRAP:	A) ☐ Bridle	B) ☐ Eastern prince	C) ☐ Horse bone
2	FUNAMBULIST:	A) ☐ Fool	B) ☐ Sleepwalker	C) ☐ Tightrope walker
3	CALABASH:	A) ☐ Gourd	B) ☐ War club	C) ☐ Musical instrument
4	FULIGINOUS:	A) ☐ Stuffed	B) ☐ Sooty	C) ☐ Green
5	CALUMNY:	A) ☐ Defamation	B) ☐ Herb	C) ☐ Notoriety
6	PLETHORA:	A) ☐ Overabundance	B) ☐ Poetry	C) ☐ Percussion hammer

137

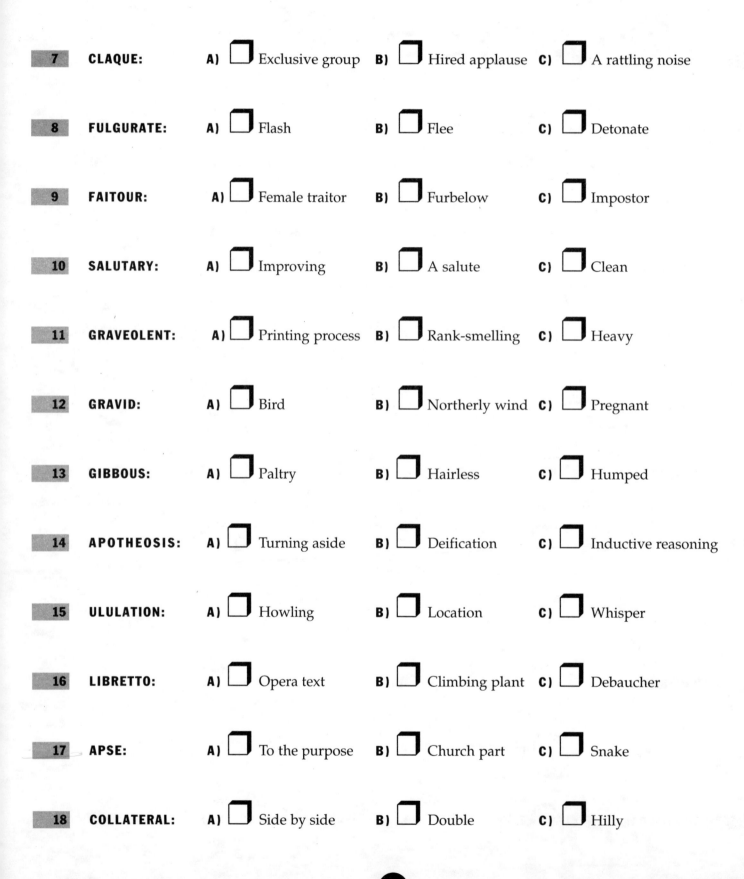

7   **CLAQUE:**   **A)** ☐ Exclusive group   **B)** ☐ Hired applause   **C)** ☐ A rattling noise

8   **FULGURATE:**   **A)** ☐ Flash   **B)** ☐ Flee   **C)** ☐ Detonate

9   **FAITOUR:**   **A)** ☐ Female traitor   **B)** ☐ Furbelow   **C)** ☐ Impostor

10   **SALUTARY:**   **A)** ☐ Improving   **B)** ☐ A salute   **C)** ☐ Clean

11   **GRAVEOLENT:**   **A)** ☐ Printing process   **B)** ☐ Rank-smelling   **C)** ☐ Heavy

12   **GRAVID:**   **A)** ☐ Bird   **B)** ☐ Northerly wind   **C)** ☐ Pregnant

13   **GIBBOUS:**   **A)** ☐ Paltry   **B)** ☐ Hairless   **C)** ☐ Humped

14   **APOTHEOSIS:**   **A)** ☐ Turning aside   **B)** ☐ Deification   **C)** ☐ Inductive reasoning

15   **ULULATION:**   **A)** ☐ Howling   **B)** ☐ Location   **C)** ☐ Whisper

16   **LIBRETTO:**   **A)** ☐ Opera text   **B)** ☐ Climbing plant   **C)** ☐ Debaucher

17   **APSE:**   **A)** ☐ To the purpose   **B)** ☐ Church part   **C)** ☐ Snake

18   **COLLATERAL:**   **A)** ☐ Side by side   **B)** ☐ Double   **C)** ☐ Hilly

19 CONCINNITY: A) ☐ Violent desire B) ☐ Private room C) ☐ Harmony

20 MORATORIUM: A) ☐ Temporary ban B) ☐ Store for corpses C) ☐ Hymn

21 DEGLUTITION: A) ☐ Removing adhesive B) ☐ Swallowing C) ☐ Debt

22 GOUT: A) ☐ Metabolic disease B) ☐ Overeating C) ☐ Pain

23 KNOUT: A) ☐ Knot B) ☐ Lump of cloth C) ☐ Whip

24 MALADY: A) ☐ Evil woman B) ☐ Illness C) ☐ Tissue of lies

25 PIPISTRELLE: A) ☐ Bat B) ☐ Flower C) ☐ Bird

26 PISTIL: A) ☐ Firearm B) ☐ Flower ovary C) ☐ Gold coin

27 RECONDITE: A) ☐ Hidden B) ☐ Explosive C) ☐ Intellectual

28 SECANT: A) ☐ Cutting B) ☐ Dried C) ☐ Angled

29 LIGNEOUS: A) ☐ Slimy B) ☐ Significant C) ☐ Wooden

30 FEDORA: A) ☐ Sailor B) ☐ Hat C) ☐ Sail

31	**INFRACOSTAL:**	A) ☐ Beneath the ribs	B) ☐ Inshore	C) ☐ Cheap
32	**LACHRYMOSE:**	A) ☐ Merry	B) ☐ Tearful	C) ☐ Shy
33	**NICTATE:**	A) ☐ Nudge	B) ☐ Blink	C) ☐ Purloin
34	**NEXUS:**	A) ☐ Junction	B) ☐ Stomach	C) ☐ Joined group
35	**PALOMINO:**	A) ☐ Horse	B) ☐ Pigment	C) ☐ Spice
36	**RADON:**	A) ☐ Gas	B) ☐ Plant	C) ☐ Heater
37	**IMPUISSANT:**	A) ☐ Tasteless	B) ☐ Smelly	C) ☐ Powerless
38	**INCUNABULA:**	A) ☐ Demons	B) ☐ Books	C) ☐ Body organs
39	**LOCUM:**	A) ☐ Deputy	B) ☐ Weight	C) ☐ Location
40	**MEIOSIS:**	A) ☐ Cell division	B) ☐ Rabbit disease	C) ☐ Poverty
41	**MORASS:**	A) ☐ Marsh	B) ☐ Lump	C) ☐ Drink
42	**CRICOID:**	A) ☐ Golden	B) ☐ Ring-shaped	C) ☐ Bent

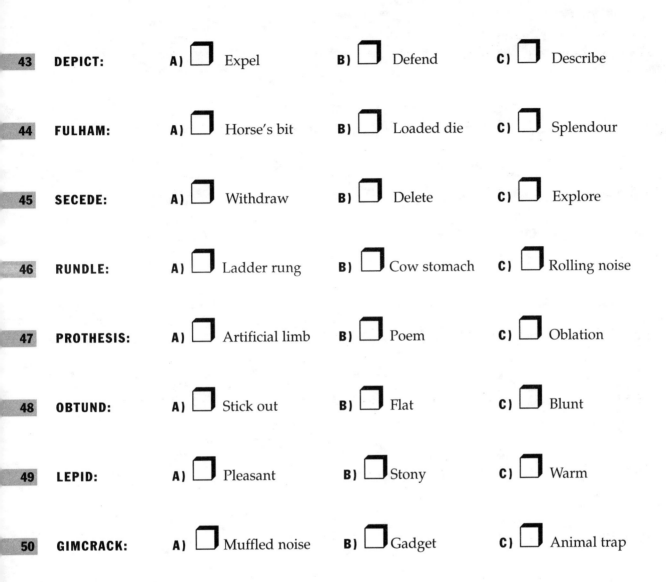

43 **DEPICT:** A) ☐ Expel B) ☐ Defend C) ☐ Describe

44 **FULHAM:** A) ☐ Horse's bit B) ☐ Loaded die C) ☐ Splendour

45 **SECEDE:** A) ☐ Withdraw B) ☐ Delete C) ☐ Explore

46 **RUNDLE:** A) ☐ Ladder rung B) ☐ Cow stomach C) ☐ Rolling noise

47 **PROTHESIS:** A) ☐ Artificial limb B) ☐ Poem C) ☐ Oblation

48 **OBTUND:** A) ☐ Stick out B) ☐ Flat C) ☐ Blunt

49 **LEPID:** A) ☐ Pleasant B) ☐ Stony C) ☐ Warm

50 **GIMCRACK:** A) ☐ Muffled noise B) ☐ Gadget C) ☐ Animal trap

MEMORY

Memory, even though it is not directly linked to intelligence, is a very useful function. People with a good memory are not necessarily of above-average intelligence and, of course, the absent-minded professor whose head is filled with brilliant ideas but who can never remember where he put anything has become a stereotype.

However, memory can have a bearing on how well you do in aptitude tests. For example, I have a very good memory and have stored away the methods needed to solve countless types of puzzle. Whether I could have solved the puzzles on my own will now never be known. Probably my true IQ would be hard to measure because so much of my score would be dependent on the element of memory.

For most purposes this does not matter much. The important thing for most of us is to be able to solve problems quickly and efficiently. If a good memory helps us achieve this aim, so much the better.

MEMORY: TEST 1

Here are a couple of memory tests. The first is a variant of a "memory" game which children play at parties. You have to look at the stationery items in the diagram for one minute, then cover up the diagram and write down as many items as you can remember.

MEMORY: TEST 2

The second test is more difficult and if you do well at this one you do indeed have a good memory. You have 1 minute 30 seconds to look at these kitchen items and then cover the diagram and write down as many as you remember.

MECHANICAL ABILITY

The actions of machines, which are governed strictly by logic, should be easily predictable by the application of a little intelligence. However, if you have ever stood for three hours by the roadside trying to fix your rebellious car you will realize that mechanical ability can often elude otherwise intelligent people. The following tests will investigate your appreciation of mechanical devices. Look at these two diagrams of machines, and answer the accompanying question.

TEST 1

If A comes first which cog will make the most turns in any given period?

TEST 2

If A moves in the direction indicated, in which direction does B move?

FORESIGHT

This is a test to see how well you are able to analyze complex information as it presents itself. Speed and accuracy are both important. The diagrams are similar to mazes, but the idea is that you should be able to find your way from A to B without running your finger or a pencil along the correct path. Time yourself and see how quickly you can find the solution by eye alone.

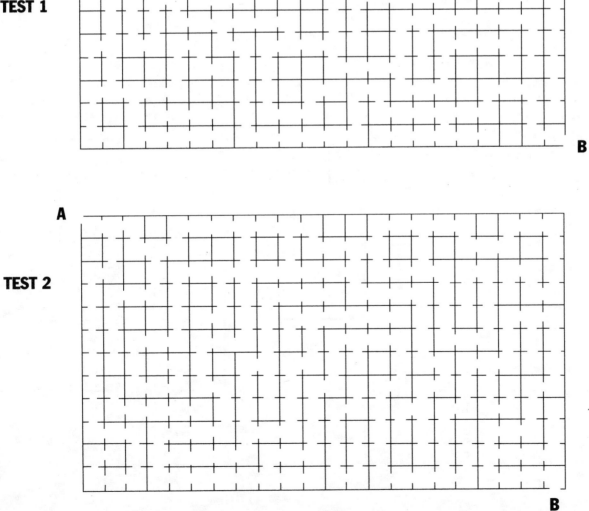

TEST 1

TEST 2

A

B

TEST 3

A

B

TEST 4

TEST 5

A

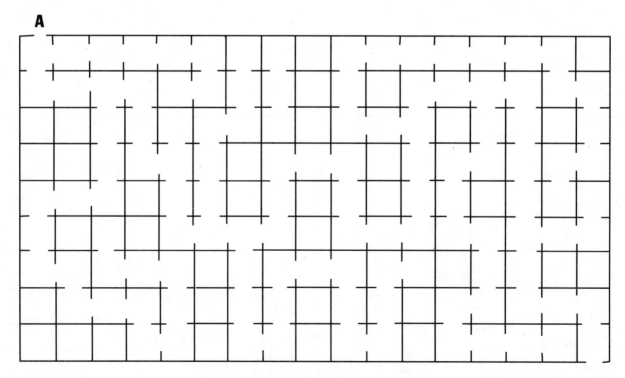

B

ATTENTION TO DETAIL

Close attention to details which may be fiddly and uninteresting can often be a vital part of a job. Many people find that, though they may be proficient at handling the broad outlines of a task, they fall down on the little things. The test below is designed to find out just how detail-conscious you are. You may find it maddeningly tedious. You may give up in disgust. But if you can stick with it and sort out every last detail, it will be you that the rest of the office turns to when the chips are down.

1 *How many balls lie within three shapes?*

2 *How many balls lie within the triangle but not within the square?*

3 *How many balls lie within the circle and the square?*

4 *How many balls lie within four-sided figures, not counting those that also lie within the circle or the triangle?*

5 *How many balls are there in total, excluding those that lie within the circle and triangle?*

CONCENTRATION

Determine your ability to concentrate by underlining each pair of letters consecutive in the alphabet when read from beginning to end. Work as quickly as possible but do not allow your mind to wander or your eyes to scan other parts of the table or you may miss some!

TIME LIMIT: 15 MINUTES

1. AGRTFGJYOPQBFGTYZDWABGYTILMNEPKRDEWFRGTUVKLNTO
2. BDTHOPXZDQYWSTJLWUSEIFHJPLWXTUDHEPQACYOISNXHYZ
3. HRBSUASOADEYUSONXLMOPGWUZBCGHUOPLMDJICNOAPLSNI
4. SHIEONFUVIKAMQLPZHDUIFOVMNDIOFMEITOPCHDSUISNCD
5. JRUDIFPVNIGLMTUIONDGEBACEGSYTIOPFNMIJBFROPTMAH
6. ANSDFPFLMTIPSNVTRSDIPMFGHJLNFHEOPWLMZXQWOXQNFG
7. BDIEOFPMLHIOPQSUIODBCHZIMTHOPWMNABSJEVIOPBMIWO
8. QGSYUEOIDPCNJFYTLPUWBSXUOPBFUROEWLMHZGIWKNDNFK
9. UKLMOQTUIEBIOSPKCNVHRUIPKMACEFGRIOPQSTWXZYIOSP
10. AJSOPWLMVUIGOPUVYZHIOPWMINSVYURIOPALMVRIOPLAMX
11. AJDOFTOPMCDGIOSHKLDWTEUOPLAHDJKEOPBCFHKRZQGTPN
12. PMSTUIPELMSHFTYIUOXJCBJKAIHIOANOEFWYQPLMSJHCUI
13. CYUOIOKSNCYUOITUOPWTUPBEDHJKTLDJKXCSDEHIOPQLAK
14. QREOMDUFITONVFGMAIOSPXYERUIHFHJIIUYZYZJFIOEPEM

15 BDFTUWOPDKMVNIOPLACHEUIPTBUSOXKCNUIDOIUHIOPRSF

16 JSIOWPLFMGBHRYUWIOAOZJBCHUISTJKSUWOPSLNCBVYIEK

17 EFQJLEMSUPOTUQHJWKLMAPALMPWXAIJWMDJOYUDBQSEIOU

18 SWVDUTHGHFWPOLMVSQUOESJDXZTRSTIGOMNGKLBVCABIFK

19 EUTODEUTCDFGSIOAPMDNEUIOPLSJQEWVVWTJGUIOHPLFGMN

20 RSWOPRLMFBUIOAKLCHEYUOWINVBIOWBYRTSBXIOBCADGEF

21 OPRSDENDHTUIOPQLMDUEIOPOSJVCYUIEDJHJIJDEHFBROP

22 EOPWLMDBFUTIOAWPSYZWKLODPFGRIOKBJHEFHIPQSTIUFO

23 EOPWLMFHTUSVXBDEQLSMIOTPLHIOVWAHSJXURIOPKMFJDI

24 PQOEKFMGHUIIHOPRSJIOPLMNGYUIOVSYTUIOPNOKMNSIWO

25 EIODPFMGJTIOPVBCHWUIROPEFABSWOQPLMFTIREOJBHEIS

26 WDJGFNHTIOPOPAJCBHFUHIOQSJHFYUIBOMFNOSTWFCNVJU

27 QIEOPEKFMNVDEHSIOPDLNCHUEIOPWPFHUIJQPWOIRJFNHF

28 OIOWPLMSBCHYRUIOEFSRSTGKHIJSQVWGDHURIOPLAMXYHI

29 QIWOPOELKFNQOWPOLFMTHSTWIOPFKLQWCNTUROPQSJEFIT

30 LUWIODPQXYDIVONKFHBVJKAQMXBCEOPTLHUYINXQHSAKFU

31 EUIWORIJVNOWLDORPHNYZQRSIEOPGMHKYLVEIDUVSTJENF

32 WIEOPLMDEIGHTJIOPSKDBGFRHTUSTWJFKIBOPWXACEGTKJ

33 EIRHIHLMHTYUISJDBFVEQREFTUIHOPLSMCEUFIORJKANDM

34 QUWIOEPKFNGBTUCJOFOBKJKWXSFJHIONPKLNBNUITOPXAM

35 VIEORTPHKMNDBGJRUOIEPWPLKASHEUFROTPMHBVCDJEUOW

36 WURHFBFVEMDKOPSLMDBVGFHRUEIOIPWSABSWOFPLJBHGYO

37 TUOGPNJQOPSLEMNFBTHURIOGPOBMJSKJDHUVIJWOEPQBCD

QUESTIONNAIRES

38 YPWIRJBVMFGIJEFNVCMSLWOPEJTHGIJSEHFBROPLSJEUFI

39 SGEYURITPMVDHCJLEKUIGQGSHWUEOPNVFEFACSTUGIOEFS

40 QUEIWOPFHJBKLFEKTLHMNGRUEIOQLSGEUTOFJNVWAHSJEF

41 LIWJMRVFJIYPTLJHVUIPOABWHDFGHKENBIJEOPFLJDUIJB

42 FEIFOPMVCDEIOHJKYLTMYZACAGABSJHFUIROLJHUFGWIOD

43 CDHFJRKLYOPXEFHJKBNRSAJDJKEIROPTLMGBVJIFKODOFU

44 WIROGPKMNJIOFGEJXCDHFURIOGHKOIWPEOUVNFKDOIMNYT

152

COMMENTARIES

Once again, we should stress that Lifeplan is a purely personal exercise with no right or wrong answers. By carefully analyzing your answers, you will gain an insight into how you feel about your current job and what you would ideally like to do. If you feel like a fish out of water at work, perhaps you need to rethink your whole career. Are you tied to a formal, 9 to 5 office working environment when you would much rather be doing something more creative? Would you rather shine as an individual, or are you quite happy being part of a team? Is money your main motivation and what are you prepared to do to earn it? The Lifeplan should help you to focus on certain aspects of your career and help you to put your current situation into context. However you use the information, the main purpose of completing this test is to crystallize for yourself your desires and expectations, and the ways in which you believe that these may be realized.

CAREER OR VOCATION?

This is how the scoring system works. The test is divided into a number of dimensions and each answer is marked as either positive or negative. If you have answered Yes to a positive question, give yourself 1 point, if you have answered No to a negative question also give yourself 1 point. If you answer a positive question with a No or a negative question with a Yes, give yourself no points. The maximum number of points you can score on each dimension is 10.

SCORING:

1. ARTISTIC/CREATIVE DIMENSION
   5+ 16+ 27+ 34- 42+ 52+ 59- 63+ 81+ 87-

2. PRACTICAL\MECHANICAL DIMENSION
   2+ 4+ 20+ 35+ 54+ 56+ 84+ 90+ 100+ 105+

3. SCIENTIFIC DIMENSION
   8+ 18+ 46+ 51+ 61+ 70+ 77+ 106+ 113+ 119+

4. ADMINISTRATIVE/CLERICAL DIMENSION
   3+ 14- 39+ 72+ 79+ 96+ 108+ 114- 116+ 118-

5. CARING/HELPING DIMENSION
   9+ 28+ 41+ 48- 74+ 91+ 98+ 101- 103+ 107-

6. LOGICAL/COMPUTATIONAL DIMENSION
   1+ 12+ 21+ 30- 33+ 68- 78+ 92+ 102+ 112-

7. PERSUASIVE DIMENSION
   15+ 26+ 47+ 62+ 64+ 97+ 99+ 104+ 109+ 117+

8. NEED FOR EXCITEMENT
   10- 22- 36+ 50+ 65+ 75+ 76+ 82+ 86+ 111+

9. STABILITY
   6+ 17+ 32- 43- 57+ 71- 89- 93+ 110- 116-

10. NEED FOR CHANGE
   23+ 25+ 37+ 45+ 55+ 60- 69+ 88- 95- 120+

11. NEED FOR PEOPLE
   13- 31- 38- 40+ 49+ 66- 80+ 83- 85+ 94+

12. NEED FOR CONTROL
   7- 11+ 19- 24+ 29+ 44+ 53+ 58+ 67- 73+

You should now be able to see how you rate on each of the dimensions and what that means for your career. For example, if you have a high score on Artistic/Creative, Need for Excitement, Need for People, and Need for Change, but you actually work as a cashier in a bank, the need for a change would be strongly indicated. On the other hand, someone who had high scores on Practical/Mechanical, Stability, and Need for Control might well be looking at an engineering career.

APTITUDE TEST A-NUMERICAL ABILITY

Basic mathematical ability is necessary in all walks of life. Even if your choice of career does not contain an obvious mathematical element as in, say, accountancy, you would be unwise to assume that you can do without these skills. One of the major grumbles heard from employers is that their staff are not sufficiently numerate. Unfortunately, large numbers of people are not only partially innumerate but also numerophobic, that is to say, they actually have a fear of maths. If your score on this test was disappointing, don't just shrug it off, do something about it. There are plenty of books on the market which will train you in basic maths and, even if you hated the subject at school, you may be surprised at how you can improve your performance.

SCORE
45-49 Excellent
40-45 Good
30-40 Average
BELOW 30 Poor

SCORING:
1.17, **2.**9, **3.**276 **4.**60, **5.**A=5,B=2, **6.**20, **7.**18, **8.**56, **9.**24, **10.**86, **11.**256, **12.**112, **13.**30, **14.**17,**15.**240, **16.** 5, **17.**4, **18.**94, **19.**P=9,Q=6, **20.**5 cassettes, 72 mins, **21.**2hrs 36mins, **22.**7:15pm, **23.**45, **24.**147, **25.**3, **26.**2, **27.**25, **28.**144, **29.**261, **30.**A=4,B=7, **31.**7.2, **32.**266, **33.**62.5, **34.**16, **35.**28, **36.**9, **37.**5, **38.**49, **39.**83, **40.**3500 **41.**1053, **42.**36, **43.**83, **44.**Y=2, Z=3, **45.**K, **46.**490hrs, **47.**114, **48.**23, **49.**3.

APTITUDE TEST B-VERBAL ABILITY

This is a tough test and anything over 40 would be an outstanding score probably achieved only by crossword fanatics and people who have a fascination with words and delight in using them. A score in the 30s would indicate a very good vocabulary and this is the level which we would expect most educated professional people to achieve. A score in the 20s is still not bad, though it would indicate that your vocabulary could do with being extended. There are actually 13 words in the test which are so common that you really should know them. Any score below 13 indicates that verbal skills are not your strong point.

SCORING:
1)b; **2)**c; **3)**a; **4)**b; **5)**a; **6)**a; **7)**a; **8)**a; **9)**c; **10)**a; **11)**b; **12)**c; **13)**c; **14)**b; **15)**a; **16)**a; **17)**b; **18)**a; **19)**c; **20)**a; **21)**b; **22)**a; **23)**c; **24)**b; **25)**a; **26)**b; **27)**a; **28)**a; **29)**c; **30)**b; **31)**a; **32)**b; **33)**b; **34)**c; **35)**a; **36)**a; **37)**c; **38)**b; **39)**a; **40)**a; **41)**a; **42)**b; **43)**c; **44)**b; **45)**a; **46)**a; **47)**c; **48)**c; **49)**b; **50)**b.

MEMORY

Memory is useful in most professions, but obviously more essential for some than others. If you had a poor score the good news is that you can improve your memory by doing regular memory exercises, or you can employ the use of memory aids such mnemonics. There are plenty of books on the market that deal with improving your memory.

SCORE
Test 1
10 excellent
8-9 quite good
Below **7** poor

Test 2
15 excellent
10-14 very good
5-9 not bad
Below **5** poor

MECHANICAL ABILITY

A little thought should give most people the answers to both these problems. If you find that you are quite unable to unravel the workings of a simple machine, rest assured that you are not alone, but banish all thoughts of a career in the automotive industry.

TEST 1: A

TEST 2: Clockwise

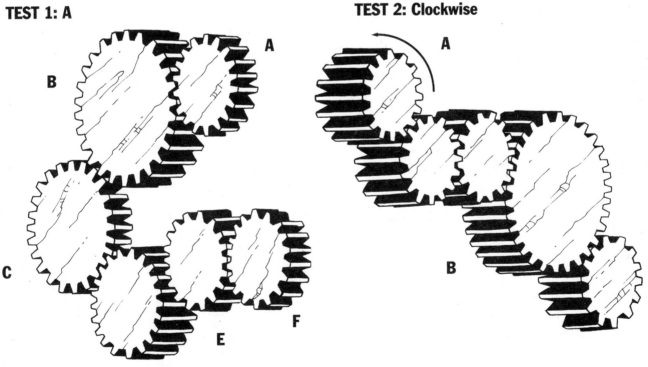

FORESIGHT

You should be able to complete these mazes in just a couple of minutes each. However they may be trickier than they look at first sight. There is no simple way to mark this test. Only you will know how quickly you got to the end and whether you did it without cheating.

ATTENTION TO DETAIL

There is no time limit for this task so with the right degree of persistence, you should have all the answers correct. However some people are just incapable of concentrating on such a fiddly task. A score of 5 is, of course, excellent, and 3 or 4 is quite acceptable for people who do not need to do much detailed work. Anything below 3 suggests that you should stick resolutely to the wider issues and let others take care of the smaller details.

SCORE:
1)4; 2)6; 3)4; 4)10; 5)10.

CONCENTRATION

This task seems deceptively simple, but because of its repetitive and tedious nature, it is easy to make mistakes. This is really quite a severe test, and if you found all 302 pairs you have done exceedingly well. The trouble with jobs demanding intense concentration is that second best will rarely do. For example, how would you like to be in the hands of an air traffic controller or a surgeon with only moderate powers of concentration? Therefore we will not bother to give lesser scores. Instead, here is a plan for improving your concentration. Find some small object that you like the look of - it doesn't matter too much what it is, but it should have plenty of interesting detail to it. Sit comfortably in a chair and examine the object in minute detail. Do this for a couple of minutes, then put the object to one side, close your eyes and try to visualize it in as much detail as possible. At first the image will fade very quickly, but with practice, you will find that you can hold a reasonably detailed picture in your mind's eye for as long as you want. When you have mastered this technique try applying your new found powers of concentration to tasks which will help to improve your skill. Very large jigsaw puzzles are excellent for this purpose.

SCORE
Total number of pairs: **302**
No. per line:
1)1 2)11 3)6 4)8 5)5 6)6 7)7 8)8 9)2 10)9 11)10 12)7 13)8 14)9 15)5 16)6 17)4 18)5 19)7 20)7 21)6 22)11 23)9 24)7 25)11 26)6 27)5 28)5 29)11 30)8 31)5 32)8 33)9 34)7 35)6 36)2 37)3 38)8 39)6 40)5 41)5 42)6 43)7 44)9 45)6.

HOW
CREATIVE
ARE YOU?

Creativity is one of those maddening aspects of human activity which is not well understood. Some psychologists insist that it is closely linked to intelligence but there are plenty of examples of people with great creative ability who are of average, or even below average, intelligence. One thing is sure, inspiration does not strike until you have put in sufficient mental effort. If you wrestle hard enough with the following tests, you may find that genuinely creative solutions will emerge.

VISUAL ARTISTIC ABILITY

Aesthetic appreciation is an ability which does not seem to depend upon intelligence. This test is not designed to see whether you could be an artist but rather looks at your ability to understand the factors, such as perspective, which influence artistic judgement. Look at the picture on the right and try to find the artist's eight deliberate errors. There is no time limit.

HOW CREATIVE ARE YOU?

Look at the diagrams below and try to write down as many interpretations for each as possible. You may view them from any angle. It sounds easy and nearly everyone will be able to come up with a few "stories" to go with each picture, however the trick is to persist beyond the obvious and try to reach into the corners of your mind and squeeze out those really original interpretations.

1

2

3

4

5

6

7

8

9

10

11

12

13

14

CREATIVE SENTENCES

Make a proper English sentence using as many words as possible from each of the groups of words below. A sentence can be formed using all of the words in each set occasionally using commas but never colons or semi-colons.

A) EASY SECTION

TIME LIMIT: MAXIMUM OF 10 MINUTES TO COMPLETE THIS SECTION.

1   slowly the crawled night the through the cat undergrowth during

2   broke people a drenched the suddenly and out all storm

3   deafeningly computer a the unexpectedly up bang with blew loud

4   hastily was block scare office the following a cleared bomb

5   overhead the flew thin low shook plane when walls the

6   as the cutting everyone reviews not predicted had were as

B) INTERMEDIATE SECTION

TIME LIMIT: MAXIMUM OF 20 MINUTES.

1   fire out smouldering was even hours the blast from massive been ago though several had the still the put rubble

2   sky the rain ominously down day the darkened evening pour had during the began it heavy was but before to

3   changed they one together as joint arranged on to broken had a trip everything go celebration when was engagement a but

4   would dinner success be events that nobody the party a turn a take better anticipated but did real the for

5 illness were kept under the mystery until to observation so doctors diagnose her in unable improved they things had her

6 extraordinary as around hoping lone some place wandered if they event couple the were take aimlessly for grounds the to

C) COMPLICATED SECTION

TIME LIMIT: MAXIMUM OF 50 MINUTES.

1 particularly event simply how troubles she know was week's solely consequences heart the responsible could knew the she not the did she disastrous for since that handle of at she

2 emergency hitting anyone up of possible fairly an results hard though was storm refuge than the victims the more were set so economically predictable had that far damaging the dreamed

3 until parent's broke children and house of despite they excitement loose managed the about the wild the with old when over to party all ran their protests just the day the

4 concerning all week possible was discussed of permission been and over building precise great considered the at granted the length for the details until had plan the arguments the not

5 claiming workplace a been due the major ongoing which negligence everyone the gross rather despite the accidental in police had assumed that concern arguments otherwise the was to than death

6 time lot decision upheavals many change lifestyle her and unwelcome which a took since going financial caused considerable on the courage simultaneously were dramatically hardship other of to especially her

STORY-TELLING

Combine the six points in each section into an outline for a continuous narrative, using all the points in whatever order.

TIME LIMIT: A MAXIMUM OF 15 MINUTES TO COMPLETE EACH SECTION.

EASY SECTION

1 You walk into the garden one morning and find water all over one particular area of the lawn.

2 At work you are criticized for taking too long to do certain tasks, and not according to instructions.

3 Friends living in a rural area suddenly telephone to cancel a dinner date you had arranged months ago.

4 In the evening you have to dispose of a collection of tiny corpses.

5 You walk into work with everyone staring at you in astonishment.

6 A friend arrives with armloads of paper kitchen towels, and dashes immediately to your kitchen.

INTERMEDIATE SECTION

1 The police arrive, demanding a list of your valuable possessions and end up staying for hours.

2 You are forced to have a long and unexpected walk home, the result of which drains your finances dramatically.

3 When you get home you are startled to find many recognizable people sitting in your living room.

4 You spend a painless, stressful and unexpected evening in the hospital emergency unit.

5 You end up booking yourself in to the local motel for the night, even though you can barely afford it.

6 You collapse on the floor at home overwhelmed completely with both joy and grief.

CHALLENGING SECTION

1   A young girl rushes past you in the street crying uncontrollably.

2   You wake up with a horrendous headache despite having consumed no alcohol the previous evening.

3   An unexpected phone call totally destroys your lifestyle and leaves you in a state of shock.

4   You leave the library feeling intensely frustrated and depressed.

5   You intentionally miss the train you bought a ticket for, and buy another one instead.

6   You spend several hours in the manager's office in a department store a long way from home.

CREATE A SOLUTION

Find a solution to each of the following problematic situations, using your creative skills to make the most of what's available.

TIME LIMIT: 5 MINUTES PER QUESTION

1   You're stuck in a windowless locked room with nobody around and the key is on the other side of the door. The room is practically empty, with a hairpin, an empty glass jar and a newspaper in the corner. How do you get out without damaging the room?

2   You swerve off the road in your car during a blackout in the Second World War. The car ends up in a small lake, but by some stroke of luck, comes to a halt on the island in the middle. You cannot swim, are totally on your own, and the car is wedged firmly into the island. How do you reach the shore without struggling unduly?

3   You are stuck on a desert island with a desperate thirst. The sun is shining brightly and there's no fresh water, no prospect of rain, and you cannot drink the sea water. You find a dilapidated wooden trunk containing a tennis racket, a book, a pan, a deflated football, two empty wine bottles, an inner tube from a bike wheel, and a fob watch. How do you get a drink?

4   You go on a picnic by a shallow river, hoping to catch some fish to eat, but when you get there, you discover you have forgotten your fishing gear. However, you have a plastic bottle full of cola, a loaf of bread, a bread knife and a blanket. How do you catch some fish?

165

ORIGAMI

The ancient Japanese art of paper-folding takes on a new look in this test of your creative powers. Using a sheet of plain paper, and without scissors, glue, paper clips or any other artificial aid, you must make each of the figures shown below. The objects you must construct are a hat, a box, and a penguin. As you see, we have given no instructions to show you how to achieve your aim, only an indication of what the finished product should look like.

TIME LIMIT: MAXIMUM OF 20 MINUTES.

LATERAL THINKING

Think of as many uses as possible for the following objects.

TIME LIMIT: 5 MINUTES PER ITEM

A HARD BOILED EGG.

_____

_____

A PAPER CLIP.

_____

_____

A KEY.

_____

_____

A NEWSPAPER.

_____

_____

A ROLL OF TINFOIL.

_____

_____

AN EMPTY GLASS BOTTLE.

_____

_____

A WASTE PAPER BASKET.

_____

_____

A BALLOON.

_____

_____

A WOODEN OAR.

_____

_____

A LEAF.

_____

_____

A LIPSTICK.

_____

_____

A WIRE COATHANGER.

_____

_____

TANGRAM

If you have ever played the ancient Chinese game of Tangram, the following test should be quite simple. Or is it? We have introduced a small variation to the traditional game in order to put your creativity to the test. Cut out the 15 geometrical pieces shown below and use them to make the following pictures: a cat, a boat, a man with a hat, a dog. You MUST use at least 13 of the pieces for each figure.

TIME LIMIT: 15 MINUTES

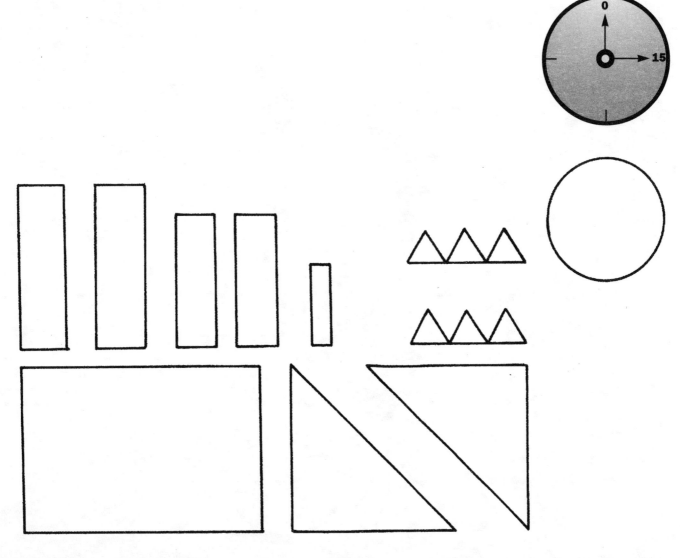

VISUALIZATION

Being able to visualize is a knack which seems to be quite independent of intelligence. Some people cannot do it at all while others find that it comes naturally. We have constructed three tasks which will test your ability to visualize.

TEST 1

Each of the diagrams below presents you with the same task. You must decide how many sides each figure has got.

TIME LIMIT: 5 MINUTES.

TEST 2

Now try a rather different approach. Look at each of the five diagrams in turn and decide which of the possible choices is a perfect match. Success depends on your ability to pick up each figure in your mind's eye and turn it until you are sure whether it is a perfect match or not.

TIME LIMIT: 10 MINUTES.

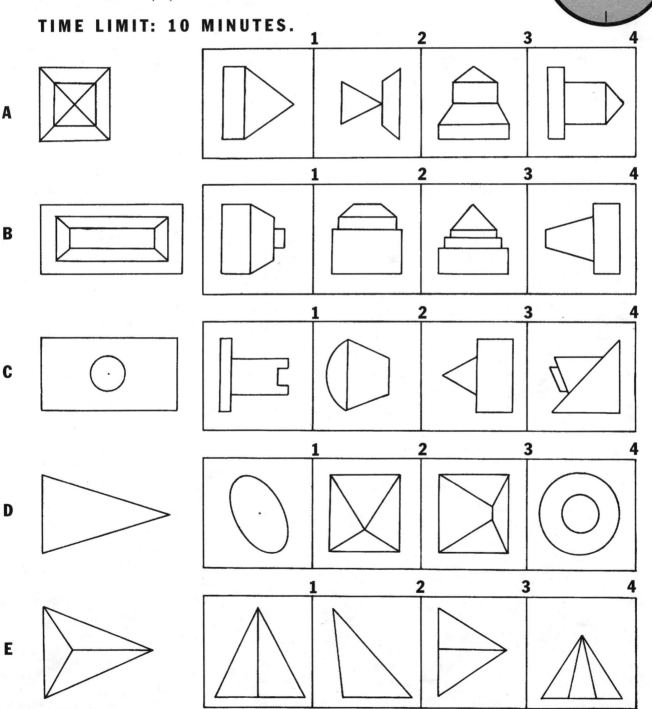

TEST 3

Here is yet another way of testing visualization. Each figure contains a hole into which you have to fit one of the other figures shown. Only one of them will be a perfect fit.

TIME LIMIT: 10 MINUTES.

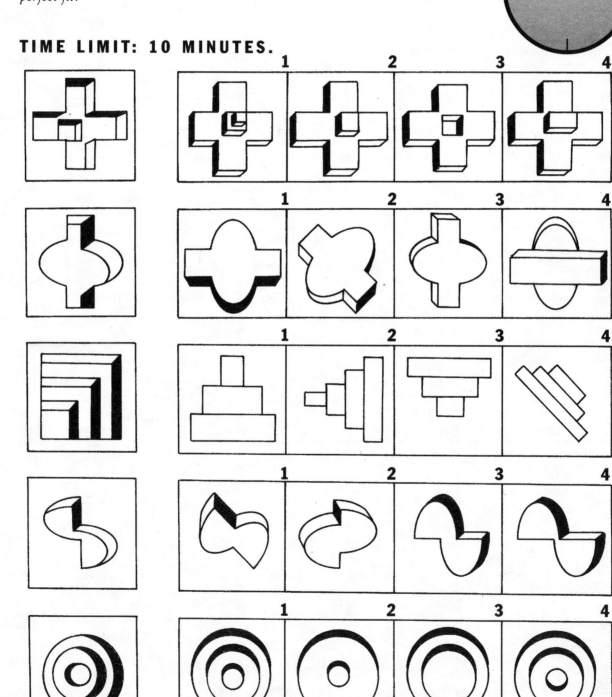

COMMENTARIES

VISUAL ARTISTIC ABILITY

Aesthetic appreciation is one of those skills which, though it can be improved with training, seems to be largely innate. Some people have no difficulty in spotting errors of symmetry, perspective and composition, others are blind to them. This test had eight errors that, according to our artist, should have been obvious to anyone with a feeling for aesthetics. If you found eight, and fairly quickly, then aesthetics is obviously your strong point. Missing one or two is just about acceptable. However if you got five or less, you would be unwise to make any aesthetic judgements that matter without the advice of an expert.

HOW CREATIVE ARE YOU?

Theoretically IQ and creative powers are fixed in infancy and cannot be increased, however it is widely recognized that regular practise does help to utilize your abilities to the full and you may therefore experience an apparent increase. Normally such tests as these would have a time limit, but in this instance this seems artificial and unnecessary. To get truly creative solutions takes time - it is much better to get a good solution eventually than a lot of average ones quickly. Most people will be able to come up with three or four explanations for each diagram. The true test of whether you are creative is if you can spot an unusual angle which other people have not thought of before.

CREATIVE SENTENCES

Creativity is a strange, unpredictable skill. Sometimes you may labour for hours or days and get nothing, only to find that the answer comes to you in a flash. However, it seems that inspiration never strikes until the preliminary brain-racking has been endured. If you enjoy this sort of effort then a creative career is indicated. If, however, for you, creative exercises feel like trying to squeeze blood from a stone (and failing), maybe you should consider another line of work.

SCORE:
161 - 180: Outstanding.
141 - 160: Very creditable.
121 - 140: Average.
101 - 120: Quite poor.
Below 100: Awful.

SCORING:
For each sentence, a maximum of 10 points can be scored, with one point subtracted for each word that is not used, giving a maximum total score of 180 points, and a minimum of 0. Below are some suggested answers:

A)

1 The cat crawled slowly through the undergrowth during the night.

2 Suddenly a storm broke out and drenched all the people.

3 The computer blew up unexpectedly with a deafeningly loud bang.

4 The office block was hastily cleared following a bomb scare.

5 The thin walls shook when the plane flew low overhead.

6 The reviews were not as cutting as everyone had predicted.

B)

1 The rubble was still smouldering from the massive blast even though the fire had been put out several hours ago.

2 The sky had darkened ominously during the day but it was evening before the heavy rain began to pour down.

3 They had arranged to go on a trip together as a joint celebration but when one engagement was broken, everything changed.

4 Nobody anticipated that the dinner party would be a real success but events did take a turn for the better.

5 The doctors were unable to diagnose her mystery illness so they kept her in under observation until things had improved.

6 The lone couple wandered aimlessly around the grounds as if they were hoping for some extraordinary event to take place.

C)

1 She simply did not know how she could handle the consequences of the disastrous event, particularly since she knew, at heart, that she was solely responsible for the week's troubles.

2 The results of the storm, though fairly predictable, were far more economically damaging than anyone had dreamed possible, hitting the victims so hard that an emergency refuge was set up.

3 The children just about managed to withhold their excitement until the day of the party when they broke loose and ran wild all over the house, despite the parent's protests.

4 Permission was not granted for the building until all the possible arguments concerning the precise details of the plan had been considered and discussed at great length over the week.

5 Everyone assumed, despite the ongoing arguments claiming otherwise, that the death was accidental rather than due to the gross negligence in the workplace which had been a major police concern.

6 The unwelcome decision to dramatically change her lifestyle took a lot of time and courage especially since many other upheavals were going on simultaneously which caused her considerable financial hardship.

STORY TELLING

SCORING:
Get a friend or relative to read through your plots, awarding a mark out of 10 for a plausible and interesting narrative, whose points smoothly link together. If no one is available to judge, do it yourself - but honestly! For each point omitted subtract 2 points from your score out of 10. The three scores added together give you your total, with a maximum score of 30.

SCORE:
26 - 30: Excellent - consider writing a novel.
21 - 25: Very good.
16 - 20: Quite acceptable.
11 - 15: Poor.
Below 10: Very low creative ability.

CREATE A SOLUTION

If you are sufficiently ingenious you will have discovered a number of ways to solve each problem. Here are our suggestions but, if you have discovered better ones, then accept our congratulations and set out adventuring with complete confidence in your ability to cope imaginatively with whatever emergencies you discover.

SCORING:
Give yourself 2 points for solving the problem in full, whether it coincides with the suggested answers or not, 1 point if you have a vague plan but cannot quite carry it out, and nothing for complete failure.

SCORE:
9 or 10: Excellent creative and practical skills.
7 or 8: Good, but take a survival kit if you go exploring.
5 or 6: Average creative abilities.
4 or below: Poor - don't go adventuring alone unless equipped for all possible emergencies!

POSSIBLE ANSWERS

1   Slide a sheet of newspaper under the door then unfold the hairpin and use it to push the key onto the paper. Pull the paper and key back under and unlock the door.

2   Extract the inner tube from the spare tyre, then float across the water in it, using your hands as paddles.

3   Start a fire by focusing a pinpoint of sunlight through the glass of the fob watch onto some paper, then set light to wood ripped from the trunk. Insert one end of the inner tube into a bottle full of sea water, put the other end in the other bottle and seal both openings with wet sand. Put the full bottle over the fire, and wait for the water to boil and distil into the other.

4   Drink or empty out the cola, then cut the bottle roughly in half with the knife so the bottom end is slightly bigger. Put some bread in the larger half then, with the lid removed, invert the end which was the top, fitting it inside the other so small fish can swim in but are unable to get out. Place it in the river, lodging it in with rocks, and wait!

ORIGAMI

It is impossible to give a scoring system for this test. Only you will ever know how close your models came to looking like the real thing. If you managed a close resemblance to all three models give yourself a pat on the back. Two out of three is still quite good. If you couldn't even make the paper hat you'd better stick to painting by numbers.

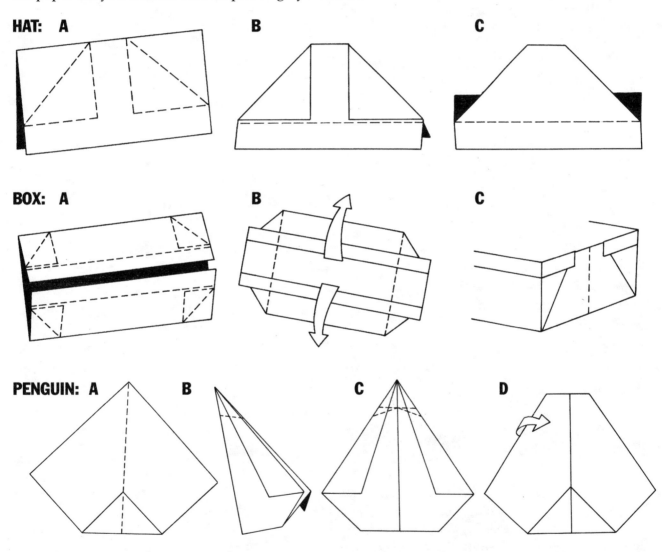

HAT: A   **B**   **C**

BOX: A   **B**   **C**

PENGUIN: A   **B**   **C**   **D**

LATERAL THINKING

SCORING:
Count the number of uses you find for each thing, scoring individually.

SCORING
16 or more: Brilliant
11-15: Quite impressive.
6-10: Good
Below 5: Low creativity.

TANGRAM

It is not easy to make all the parts of the picture look as if they serve some believable function. Give yourself 10 points for completing a picture and subtract a point for each piece you have left over. A total of 40 would be superb and puts your creative powers beyond doubt. Anything over 30 is quite creditable. A score in the twenties would be average. If you score below 15 then creativity is perhaps not your strong point.

VISUALIZATION

Visualization is a very useful skill but it is one which does not necessarily go hand-in-hand with intelligence (though visualization exercises are often included in IQ tests). However, observation shows that some highly intelligent people simply cannot pick an object up in their mind's eye, manipulate it, and then draw conclusions from the experience or visualize how a problem should be solved.

SCORING:
TEST 1: 1) 10; **2)** 5; **3)** 8; **4)** 30; **5)** 15: **6)** 10; **7)** 18 **8)** No sides, the figure is hollow
TEST 2: A) 3 **B)** 4 **C)** 3 **D)** 1 **E)** 1
TEST 3: A) 2 **B)** 1 **C)** 3 **D)** 2 **E)** 4

SCORES: TEST 1
6-8 Very good
3-5 Good
Under **3** Poor

TEST 2
5 Very good
3-4 Good
Under **3** Poor

TEST 3
5 Very good
3-4 Good
Under **3** Poor

THE
REAL YOU

How well do you know yourself? What do others think of you? Are you assertive, socially adept and good with people, or a bit shy and reserved? Insight into what makes us tick is something most of us desire but find hard to obtain. This section is aimed at giving you a look at the forces that motivate you. You are the world's most qualified person on matters to do with your own psyche and, with help from these tests, you should be able to compile a fascinating self-assessment that will help you understand the way you behave.

ASSERTIVENESS

How assertive are you, and are you more assertive in some situations rather than others? Tick the appropriate answers below.

1 **You buy a new shirt, get home, and find it has a small hole in the back. Do you:**
A) Treat it as just one of those things. ❑
B) Return to the shop, demanding a refund. ❑
C) Wander into the shop, produce the shirt, and leave with little more than an apology. ❑

2 You have been waiting for 10 minutes to be served in a bar when a man saunters to your side and is served instantly. Do you:
A) Loudly call out that you were first. ☐
B) Cast the barman a withering glance and determine to be served next. ☐
C) Return to your seat without a drink, intending to get one later. ☐

3 You visit an expensive restaurant for your birthday, but the service is atrocious, and food awful. Do you:
A) Grumble about it with your friends, and refuse to go there again. ☐
B) Demand to see the manager, insisting on a substantial reduction. ☐
C) Pretend that everything was wonderful. ☐

4 Someone lights a cigarette in your no-smoking office. Do you:
A) Try to ignore it and continue working. ☐
B) Cough noisily. ☐
C) Escort the smoker outside to finish the cigarette. ☐

5 Your train to work is 50 minutes late for the third consecutive day. Do you:
A) Telephone the rail company, asking pointedly whether the timetable has been changed. ☐
B) Arrive at the station the following morning complete with a petition you demand everyone signs. ☐
C) Decide to take the bus instead. ☐

6 While you are on a blind date at the cinema an unwelcome arm creeps around your shoulder. Do you:
A) Squirm uncomfortably and keep silent. ☐
B) Smile a sickly smile, pretending you're enjoying every minute. ☐
C) Loudly request that the offending arm is removed. ☐

7 You do your weekly supermarket shop, but later find you have been charged for six items you did not buy. Do you:
A) Decide to watch the cashier carefully in future. ☐
B) Personally return the receipt, circling the six items, and getting a refund. ☐
C) Casually mention to the cashier the following week that you were over-charged and accept his apology. ☐

8 A friend asks you to type some work for her during your already hectic schedule. Do you:
A) Agree at once, and take it to her the following evening, having stayed up all night. ☐
B) Casually agree, but never get around to it so the friend eventually asks someone else. ☐
C) Refuse point blank, while making a joke about your busy life. ☐

9 **You are trying to give up smoking, but a friend still offers you a cigarette. Do you:**
A) Look longingly at the cigarette, but refuse it, inhaling the friend's fumes instead. ❐
B) Weakly accept, and smoke it guiltily. ❐
C) Declare proudly that you no longer smoke. ❐

10 **In a taxi, you suspect that the driver has been drinking on the job. Do you:**
A) Ask him to stop at once, then ring the taxi company to complain. ❐
B) Tell the driver you have changed your mind and can he please drop you at the next corner. ❐
C) Hold on to the seat and suffer the rest of the journey in silence. ❐

11 **You go for a job interview and are unfairly criticized for your lack of experience. Do you**
A) Apologize, but remind the interviewer of your age and qualifications. ❐
B) Politely point out how it is impossible to have worked for 5 years in various companies when you only left college 3 years ago and have been in demand ever since. ❐
C) Agree with the comments and leave the interview feeling a failure. ❐

12 **You visit a relative in hospital, and the doctor explains her condition with words you don't understand. Do you:**
A) Nod your head, claiming you understand. ❐
B) Ask the doctor to explain the terms used. ❐
C) Wait for the doctor to leave, then ask the nurse for a simple explanation. ❐

13 **You open the door to a vacuum cleaner salesman who immediately offers you a free bottle of cleaning fluid without mentioning that he is selling vacuums. Do you:**
A) Inspect the cleaning solution, and let the salesman complete his pitch before eventually telling him you're not interested. ❐
B) Offer the salesman a cup of tea, and end up buying three vacuum cleaners, two of which make "ideal gifts". ❐
C) Inform the salesman that if you wanted a new vacuum cleaner you would go to the local electrical shop and ask him to kindly stop wasting your time. ❐

14 **When sitting outside one afternoon, someone next door plays loud music which booms out of the house. Do you:**
A) Turn up your own in competition. ❐
B) Go there and politely but insistently ask for the music to be turned down. ❐
C) Go out for the day to escape from the noise. ❐

15 **A new rule is introduced at work that whoever arrives last has to make all the teas and coffees for the day. Your bus is permanently late, and you only drink cold drinks anyway. Do you:**
A) Quickly learn how to use the hot drinks machine. ❐
B) Grumble about it so much that eventually the rule is dropped. ❐
C) Explode, declaring your time is much better spent actually working, and refuse to make a single cup. ❐

16 While walking your dog another appears on the scene, with its owner far behind, and attacks your dog so badly that it requires several trips to the vet. Do you:
A) Mention your dog's injuries to the other dogwalker next time you pass each other, and accept the apology and offer of a contribution to the vet's fees. ❐
B) Take the other dogwalker's name and address, and send an invoice for all the fees, which you later collect in full. ❐
C) Walk your dog by another route, avoiding any contact with the vicious dog. ❐

17 You charter a trip only to find on arrival that the hotel backs onto a noisy road, and the beach is 20 minutes away. Do you:
A) Take the first flight home, writing several letters of complaint until you get a full refund. ❐
B) Make the most of the break, later telephoning the holiday company to express your dissatisfaction. ❐
C) Treat the traffic noise like the dawn chorus, and tell yourself how good all the walking you're doing is for you. ❐

18 You always receive a birthday card from a colleague who you know frequently spreads gossip about you behind your back. On his birthday, do you:
A) Gasp, claiming you had completely forgotten, but all the best wishes for the day anyway. ❐
B) Buy a card a month in advance, writing inside how much you enjoy your friendship. ❐
C) Spend the day refusing to acknowledge his birthday, while making pointed comments about the hypocrisy of some people. ❐

19 When sharing a flat with some friends you find that you are continually doing the clearing up. Do you:
A) Put some music on to help while away the hours spent at the sink. ❐
B) Go on strike until there are no clean utensils left, and the others start to help out. ❐
C) Mention mildly over dinner that it would be nice if someone else cleared up for a change. ❐

20 In a snack bar, you order a tuna sandwich without cucumber, and tea with sugar. You get a tuna and cucumber sandwich, and a tea without. Do you:
A) Call the waitress over, who duly brings what you initially ordered, with an apology. ❐
B) Eat up, but mention it when paying, accepting the slight discount offered for the dissatisfaction. ❐
C) Remove the cucumber, despite feeling nauseous from the smell, and gulp down the tea as quickly as possible. ❐

21 You find yourself roped into a conversation with people you do not like on a subject you know little about. Do you:

A) Remain silent, waiting for a suitable moment to slip away. ☐

B) Burst into the conversation, declaring that you have people to meet, and places to go, so goodbye. ☐

C) Bluff your way through questions, then cleverly change the subject to something which leaves the others startled, so they make their excuses and leave. ☐

22 You win a reasonable-sized prize in a lottery, which the local paper features. A heap of begging letters appears on your doorstep. Do you:

A) Throw them all away, feeling completely unruffled by the adverse publicity, declaring it's your money to use as you wish. ☐

B) Sort through the letters, sending small amounts to a few causes you feel are really worthwhile. ☐

C) Accept all the invitations to dinner, handing out your winnings to anyone who asks. ☐

23 A taxi drops you at a party and you try to pay with a note three times the cost of the journey. You have no smaller change, and the driver informs you that neither does she. Do you:

A) Tell her to keep the note, writing the money off as being your own fault for not carrying change. ☐

B) Argue furiously with the driver about how ridiculous it is that she has no change until she gets fed up and leaves without payment. ☐

C) Ask a friend at the party to lend you the change, giving it to the driver with a grimace, and no tip. ☐

24 The telephone rings just as you are serving the evening meal. Do you:

A) Answer the phone, neglecting the food, and end up eating a cold dinner. ☐

B) Talk for a few seconds, but then cut the call short, agreeing to phone back later. ☐

C) Answer the phone, immediately telling the caller what you are doing, and asking him to call later on. ☐

25 Some friends come over and put the television on to watch athletics. You intended to spend the afternoon watching a classic movie. Do you:

A) Video the movie, making your feelings clear, and watch athletics for the time being. ☐

B) Serve some drinks, and read a magazine instead. ☐

C) Switch over to the movie, and hide the control, so the others have no choice. ☐

26 A sales assistant completely ignores you waiting to be served, and continues to talk to some friends. Do you:

A) Demand to be served at once. ☐

B) Put your items back after a while, and go to another shop instead. ☐

C) Wait a few minutes, then casually ask if there's any chance of being served today. ☐

27 You mention to a policewoman that you have noticed some suspicious occurrence nearby. She rudely rejects your ideas as petty and lacking foundation. Do you:

A) Note down her number, storm to the nearest police station, and make a complaint. ❏

B) See a policeman nearby, approach him, and insist that he listens to you. ❏

C) Tend to agree, and apologize for wasting her time. ❏

28 Your sister has bought a new coat, which does not fit properly, or suit her at all. However, she loves it, and asks your opinion. Do you:

A) Say little, but later enthuse about another coat she pulls out. ❏

B) Tell her you think it looks gorgeous. ❏

C) Ask her if she's wearing it for a bet. ❏

29 You decide to risk taking a new job which contrasts with anything you have done before, and proves to be very tricky. Do you:

A) Treat it as a challenge, introducing new methods of working until you wonder why you didn't change jobs years ago. ❏

B) Resign after a few days, returning to the security of a job similar to your previous one. ❏

C) Stick it out for a couple of months before deciding it's not really for you, and start looking for something different. ❏

30 You visit a car showroom, where you want to buy a car you've had your eye on for months. The salesman, however, leads you over to another, more expensive model, and tries to persuade you to buy that. Do you:

A) Leave without buying anything, returning to the showroom when a more approachable salesman is on duty. ❏

B) Agree to buy the more expensive model, recognizing the benefits in the long run. ❏

C) Ignore the saleman's futile efforts, and purchase the car you really want. ❏

MORAL/PHYSICAL COURAGE

How brave are you? Would you rush into a burning building to rescue a trapped friend, or phone the fire service? Would you stand up for your views even if they were so unpopular that you were persecuted for them? Alternatively, perhaps you prefer to leave the heroics to others. Answer these questions and find out.

1   **While walking along the street you notice a man acting aggressively towards a young girl. Do you:**
A) Ignore it - they can sort it out between themselves. ❏
B) Approach the pair discreetly to work out whether the girl is all right, if ❏
necessary confronting the man.
C) Get a policeman. ❏

2   **You are offered a more interesting job with better prospects but without the security of your current position. Do you:**
A) Grab the new opportunity with relish because you feel you won't get anywhere ❏
without taking risks.
B) Consider the offer but decide to look for something less daunting instead. ❏
C) Decline the offer as any job is better than no job and you fear that this offer ❏
might turn sour.

3   **A local charity is in need of funds, and asks if you would do a sponsored parachute jump for their worthy cause. Do you:**
A) Ask if you could do a sponsored walk instead. ❏
B) Refuse, but donate some money to compensate. ❏
C) Start training and finding sponsors. ❏

4   **During a walk in the country, you hear a boy screaming for help and discover he has fallen into a river and cannot swim. Do you:**
A) Run to the nearest phone and telephone for an ambulance. ❏
B) Take off your shoes and dive in to help him. ❏
C) Quickly search for a large branch then edge your way into the water, telling him ❏
to grab it so you can pull him in.

5   **You've been working for a company for a considerable time and feel you are due for a salary increase but it has not been mentioned at work. Do you:**
A) Approach your boss, raising the matter politely. ❏
B) Work harder and drop hints about wages in an attempt to make your boss ❏
realize you are entitled to more money.
C) Continue as before, but look for any better paid job that comes up. ❏

6   **A fire breaks out in your office at work, and in the rush to escape, you see that a colleague is trapped under some shelves close to the flames. Do you:**
A) Rush out and inform the firefighters of your colleague's exact location and situation ☐
B) Run back, struggling with the heat and the shelves until you have freed your colleague. ☐
C) Attempt to move the shelves but dash out to inform the firefighters of the situation when you feel you cannot put your life at risk any longer. ☐

7   **A dominating relative calls you up at the last minute to say that she urgently needs you to carry out some relatively unimportant task at the weekend, but you have arranged to go out with friends. Do you:**
A) Tell her you would love to help, but firmly state that you have other arrangements. ☐
B) Ask her to wait until the following weekend, cancelling other less important arrangements of your own. ☐
C) Weakly explain that you were planning to go out, but end up agreeing to comply with her demands. ☐

8   **Out of the following list of activities, which would you prefer:**
A) Hang-gliding. ☐
B) Skiing. ☐
C) Cycling. ☐

9   **You arrive late at work for the first time having overslept, despite the alarm clock going off. In response to the demand for an explanation, do you:**
A) Say your alarm didn't go off. ☐
B) Admit that it was your own fault, and offer to stay on late. ☐
C) Become so flustered that your boss gives up asking for an explanation. ☐

10   **You're camping with a friend when you find a spider in the tent. Your friend is petrified of them, and you're not too keen either. Do you:**
A) Take a deep breath, scoop it into your hand, and drop it outside. ☐
B) Stamp on it, then put the dead spider in a cup to dispose of it. ☐
C) Scream until someone comes to your aid and gets rid of the spider for you. ☐

11   **A friend with a highly volatile nature asks your opinion on something, but you know criticism will not be welcome. Do you:**
A) Speak the truth. ☐
B) Lie. ☐
C) Give a non-committal response. ☐

12 Some extremely unconventional friends ask you to go out into town with them. Aware of the comments and stares which will greet them and you, do you:
A) Go out wearing sunglasses, a hat and any other disguise you can conjure up. ☐
B) Make some feeble excuse, preferring to stay at home instead. ☐
C) Be seen with them with your head held high. ☐

13 You see some joyriders stealing a car within footsteps of you. When it pulls away, do you:
A) Pretend you haven't seen it. ☐
B) Jump on the front of the car to try to stop it. ☐
C) Call the police from the nearest phone. ☐

14 You go out for dinner wanting to stay sober, but friends mock you for not drinking. Do you:
A) Relent, accepting the drinks offered. ☐
B) Inform them that you would like to hang on to your liver even if they don't. ☐
C) Have one or two drinks only after being pressurized. ☐

15 You get the opportunity to be the first person to land on Mars using previously untried technology. Do you:
A) Start training for the expedition. ☐
B) Absolutely refuse to go. ☐
C) See if you could go to the moon instead. ☐

16 You're due to go to the dentist but know that various things are wrong. Do you:
A) Delay going for as long as possible. ☐
B) Get the earliest possible appointment. ☐
C) Go sometime after receiving a reminder. ☐

17 A war breaks out in a nearby country and appeals for extra soldiers are launched. Do you:
A) Sign up immediately. ☐
B) Wait until fighting becomes compulsory. ☐
C) Emigrate. ☐

18 You injure your leg badly when out walking on your own, and blood and dirt seem to be everywhere. Do you:
A) Wipe it briefly, then wrap it up with some cloth so you don't have to look at it. ☐
B) Inspect and treat the wound as best you can. ☐
C) Try to ignore it until you can get someone else to treat it. ☐

19 Someone nearby cuts himself seriously. Do you:
A) Rush over with a first aid box. ☐
B) Panic about what you should do to help. ☐
C) Find someone else to deal with it. ☐

20 A member of your family needs a kidney donation, and you discover you are a suitable donor. Do you:
A) Wait to see if anyone else will come forward first. ❑
B) Go right ahead and donate one. ❑
C) Feel very reluctant to become a donor. ❑

21 You see a wild cat with an untreated broken leg. Do you:
A) Gingerly approach it, then take it to the vet. ❑
B) Get other people to help you capture it, then put a splint on it yourself. ❑
C) Inform the nearest animal welfare organization. ❑

22 You are asked to go bungie-jumping for a friend's birthday. Do you:
A) Say you'll stay on the ground and take the photos. ❑
B) Turn up early on the day so you can get the most jumps in. ❑
C) Do it once, then refuse to do it again. ❑

23 After failing your driving test four times, do you:
A) Give up, using public transport instead. ❑
B) Book some more lessons so you can retake it as soon as possible. ❑
C) Wait a few months before having the nerve to start the whole process again. ❑

24 Your friend's goldfish dies while they are away because you forgot to feed it. Do you:
A) Buy a replacement and hope they won't notice. ❑
B) Tell them as soon as they get back. ❑
C) Leave a note explaining what happened and try to avoid them. ❑

25 You see an advertizement asking for volunteers to test a new potentially life-saving drug for the first time. Do you:
A) Reply to the appeal, ignoring the risks and concentrating on the possible benefits. ❑
B) Think it stupid to get involved in such a thing. ❑
C) Consider applying if you are really strapped for cash. ❑

26 Which of the following jobs would you most mind doing:
A) Meter warden. ❑
B) Door-to-door salesperson. ❑
C) Post office clerk. ❑

27 You are attracted to someone you would like to go out with. Do you:
A) Ask him/her outright to go on a date. ❑
B) Ask a friend to ask a friend to ask him/her. ❑
C) Hope that he/she asks you. ❑

28 You are travelling near a panic-stricken third world country, desperate for medical care which you could help with, but which is also in constant danger of being attacked. Do you:
A) Avoid the area as much as possible. ❏
B) Start helping on the spot, trying to recruit other people from home to come, too. ❏
C) Drive in and then out with a car load of medical supplies. ❏

29 While walking along a cliff edge you see a man who has clearly lost his footing and is balancing precariously on a rock just below where you are. Do you:
A) Attempt to pull him up yourself with other people holding on to you. ❏
B) Run off, despite adverse weather conditions, to call for an ambulance. ❏
C) Stay and talk to him until you see someone else you can call over to help. ❏

30 You are chasing a runaway pickpocket you caught in action, and catch up with him balancing along some dangerous scaffolding on a construction site. Do you:
A) Follow without a moment's hesitation. ❏
B) Stand at the base of it, yelling at him to come down. ❏
C) You don't even venture into the site. ❏

DOING VERSUS THINKING

Are you a doer, a thinker or a well-balanced mixture? This test will help you to find out whether your first inclination is to leap into action or to sit and think about it.

1 When going to work in the car, you get stuck in a traffic jam. Do you:
A) Feel frustrated for doing nothing. ❏
B) Go off into a daydream. ❏
C) Plan your day carefully, while looking at the clock more and more often. ❏

2 When enjoying a day off, do you:
A) Rush around doing all the things you never have time for normally. ❏
B) Spend the day curled up with books and the newspaper. ❏
C) Potter about doing nothing very much and feeling bored. ❏

3 On your day off, do you:
A) Get up whenever you wake up. ❏
B) Set your alarm for 7a.m. and dash out for a run. ❏
C) Lie in bed for hours, philosophizing on the state of the world. ❏

4   **You go to a friend's house for dinner. After the meal, do you:**

A) Immediately start helping to clear away. ☐

B) Maintain the table conversation. ☐

C) Offer to help, and happily accept the refusal. ☐

5   **On a long car journey, do you:**

A) Look out of the window, read a bit, chat a bit. ☐

B) Remain completely immersed in a book. ☐

C) Drive. ☐

6   **When preparing for your vacation, do you:**

A) Spend the days before leaving finalizing preparations. ☐

B) Look at your immaculately packed suitcase for a week before you leave. ☐

C) Throw a few things together a few hours before you are due to leave. ☐

7   **During an evening at home, are you:**

A) Catching up on phone calls, letters, and various other things you've been meaning to do. ☐

B) Watching television. ☐

C) Tidying up in between popping out for a meal and reading the newspaper. ☐

8   **You live on the seventh floor of a building. Do you:**

A) Wait for the lift every day. ☐

B) Only take the stairs when the lift isn't working. ☐

C) Energetically plump for the stairs every time. ☐

9   **When asked over the telephone to carry out a piece of work which should take several hours, do you:**

A) Complete it on schedule, ready for collection after a couple of days. ☐

B) Rush it off immediately, and mail it at once. ☐

C) Finish the task in hand, and consider the new work carefully before rushing into anything. ☐

10   **Someone suggests a novel idea for a fund-raising event for a local cause. Do you:**

A) Go away and give it some thought, before discussing it with someone else. ☐

B) Seize the idea with great enthusiasm and start planning possible venues. ☐

C) Flatly declare that you are too busy to take on anything else at present, then go and watch television. ☐

11   **Some friends suggest a group outing to a nearby museum. Do you:**

A) Start making the arrangements. ☐

B) Go along quite happily with whatever is suggested. ☐

C) Tell them you are not really interested and go on your own instead to enjoy the museum fully. ☐

12   **At a party, do you:**
A) Make conversation with anyone who happens to say hello. ☐
B) Help distribute the food and drink. ☐
C) Talk, drink, and dance the evening away. ☐

13   **When just sitting around between appointments, are you:**
A) Totally content. ☐
B) Anxious to get on. ☐
C) Happy to wait for a short while. ☐

14   **A new person is moving in next door. Do you:**
A) Take some drinks over and start helping. ☐
B) When they're nearly finished, go and offer your services. ☐
C) Watch from the window. ☐

15   **Do you thrive when you have:**
A) Nothing in particular to do. ☐
B) A huge list of things that need doing. ☐
C) A few things that you can do at your leisure. ☐

16   **When choosing a holiday, would you prefer to go to:**
A) A pleasant seaside holiday resort. ☐
B) An exotic sun-kissed island. ☐
C) On a watersports and adventure break. ☐

17   **You and a colleague are set similar tasks for the day at work. Do you:**
A) Finish first. ☐
B) Stay late to finish up. ☐
C) Wind up at more or less the same time. ☐

18   **You haven't anything specific to do for the day. Do you:**
A) Feel miserable and at a loss. ☐
B) Revel in the luxury. ☐
C) After a while feel restless, and go out. ☐

19   **After completing one task, do you:**
A) Meander into another one. ☐
B) Rush enthusiastically into the next one. ☐
C) Wait until someone else tells you what to do. ☐

20   **If other people are doing what you can see to be an incompetent job of something, do you:**
A) Ignore it and get on with whatever you're doing. ☐
B) Offer advice whenever asked. ☐
C) Rush over and take charge. ☐

21   **What annoys you the most out of the following:**
A) When people rush things and make mistakes. ☐
B) When people take a very long time doing something, but do it thoroughly. ☐
C) When people never get around to doing things. ☐

22   **Which of the following would you prefer:**
A) Doing a crossword. ☐
B) Going out for a meal. ☐
C) Hiking around the countryside. ☐

23   **When confronted with a steep hill leading to a monument on a group outing, do you:**
A) Stay at the bottom of the hill and look at it through binoculars. ☐
B) Stride up the hill and inspect it at close range. ☐
C) Gaze out at the scenery around you, waiting for the others to come down. ☐

24   **At a party you are asked what you think is the purpose of life. Do you:**
A) Hand out some drinks. ☐
B) Change the subject. ☐
C) Spend the next hour debating possible answers. ☐

25   **On a close relative's birthday, do you:**
A) Bake a special cake. ☐
B) Make up a birthday poem. ☐
C) Phone for a chat. ☐

26   **You have a hectic schedule for the weekend, with loads of things to do. Do you:**
A) Concentrate on one thing at a time, gradually getting everything done. ☐
B) Dash around doing three things at once, and complete the weekend's plan on Saturday. ☐
C) Put everything off until next weekend and relax in the sun instead. ☐

27   **If you have a fully booked few days and someone asks you to do a task which will take an hour or two. Do you:**
A) Agree, and then wonder when you can do it. ☐
B) Apologize, saying you are too busy on the computer. ☐
C) Start on the task the minute you're asked. ☐

28   **Your house needs redecorating. Do you:**
A) Do it yourself. ☐
B) Pay a decorator to do it. ☐
C) Forget about it for a few months. ☐

29   **If your washing machine broke down, would you:**
A) Go to the launderette. ☐
B) Wash everything by hand for a while. ☐
C) Kick it, and hope it comes back to life. ☐

COLOR
ANALYSIS

Such is the curiosity of people to find out more about what makes them tick that over the centuries they have resorted to a multitude of methods which were supposed to provide insight into personality. Most of these methods were misguided and based upon quasi-scientific theories which did not stand up under close scientific scrutiny. Phrenology (reading character from an examination of the shape of a person's skull) was a case in point. It was widely believed in but never really worked and has long since been consigned to the dustbin of history. However, a couple of these unorthodox methods have persisted and are still in use.

Graphology, in which personality is deduced from an examination of the subject's hand-writing, is still popular with some people and enjoys something of a vogue in France, where most of the serious investigation into its use has been carried out. Psychologists object that the link which graphologists make between handwriting and personality is often based on some rather naive and arbitrary correspondence. For example, someone with forward sloping writing is said to be forceful and assertive while someone whose writing slopes backwards is regarded as shy and retiring. Graphologists insist that empirical evidence backs up such assertions, but psychologists are,

understandably, wary of accepting their claims without the benefit of further resarch.

What other methods of analysis might work? A number of scientists have expressed interest in human reaction to color and have carried out research to see whether different psychological types show different color preferences. Certainly there can be no doubt that most human beings are profoundly affected by color. Take as an example the photographs shown on the following pages. We have taken an interior shot of a room and, purely by manipulating the color balance, changed it from a warm, inviting scene into a cold and forbidding one. Nothing about the room itself has been changed at all.

The only alteration we have made is to shift the color balance from the red end of the spectrum to the blue end of the spectrum.

These reactions are commonly exploited by people trying to influence our behavior and it is extraordinary the extent to which our reactions can be manipulated by very small color changes. For example, butchers instal lighting with a pink tinge to it that will make the meat look more attractive, while greengrocers go for greenish lighting which enhances the natural green of the vegetables.

There is no doubt at all about the power color has to affect us, but does it give a clue to personality? At least some color choices are dictated by the society to which we belong. For example, in the West we think of white as the color denoting purity, virginity and cleanliness. In the Far East it is used to symbolize death and mourning. Similarly, various political movements and religious causes have adopted colors and made them their own. Thus we think of red as the color of communism, green as the color of Islam and, if you happen to be American, British or French, then a combination of red, white and blue will bring a patriotic glint to your eye.

Can you use color to influence others? Many people, though sceptical about how far it is possible to take color analysis, would accept that colors do have a psychological effect. However, what is even more controversial is the idea, strenuously promoted by some, that it is

A room decorated in colors from the red end of the spectrum has a warm and inviting feel to it.

possible to influence your own mood or that of those around you, purely by the use of color. There have already been experiments in which it is claimed that violent young offenders were calmed by placing them in rooms decorated in a peaceful shade of pink.

A well-known British color therapist, Joy Peach, tells me that changing the color of your clothes can make a marked difference to the way you feel. What is more, as it might look strange turning up at a business meeting wearing a confidence-giving red jacket, it is possible to gain the same effect by changing the color of your underwear. A pair of bright red knickers, she claims, will give you just the confidence you need to clinch that vital deal. You can also use

the technique to influence others. Writing your letter on peaceful blue paper will help to ensure a calm reception. If you want the reader to be impressed by the intellectual quality of your arguments, use yellow. At the end of a troublesome day why not put an orange light bulb in the socket and cheer yourself up? Does it work? Well, I have to admit to having had no great success with this technique but, in a spirit of scientific inquiry, why not try it yourself?

The same room decorated with colors from the blue end of the spectrum has an icy, cold feel.

COLOR PREFERENCE

Our reactions to color are very complicated. Research carried out by scientists such as Hermann Rorschach and Max Luscher has attempted to show how particular personality types are attracted to certain colors and repelled by others. When shown a collection of color swatches and asked to name a favorite color most of us will go for one of the primary colors, red and blue being the favorites. If someone shows a pronounced dislike of all colors, or is greatly attracted to white, gray or black, this may well be a symptom of some mental disturbance. Complete the test below to see what color reveals about your personality.

Use this test to establish your individual color preferences and dislikes, and what this reveals about your personality. Look at the color swatches below. First choose your favorite color, then choose your least favorite color. This selection should be made quickly and intuitively. Don't try to rationalize your choice by thinking about your clothes, home decoration, etc. You must take no longer than 30 seconds to select your colors. Once you have made your choices, look up the interpretations in the commentary.

COMMENTARIES

RED

FAVORITE

Those who like red are thought of as extroverted, happy, impulsive and sexually very active. Red lovers are said to be forceful, outgoing and assertive types who tackle life with gusto. They are thought of as leaders rather than followers and are generally very competitive. Red lovers may be ruthless in their determination to succeed and not easily thwarted. We should not lose sight of the fact that red is the color of blood and is internationally used to denote danger. Someone who is overly attracted to red may be showing signs of lack of emotional control.

LEAST FAVORITE

A pronounced dislike of red is considered very suspect. At the least it would lead one to expect a person who suffers from feelings of frustration and disappointment with life and, if it were carried to extremes, it would signify a very pronounced withdrawal from all social contact. Red is not a much-hated color.

ORANGE

FAVORITE

This is a powerful color which provokes strong reactions: you can love it or hate it but you can't ignore it! Love of orange is often thought of as indicating a sociable, friendly, outgoing character. Happy extroverts who get on well with others are typical orange lovers. It is not a color which sits easily with others and, used unwisely, will clash violently. Likewise its admirers are thought of by color analysts as people of an individualist turn of mind who do not take kindly to received wisdom but tend to go their own way. Orange lovers can react hastily and without thought, which can lead to explosive situations at home and at work which leave them emotionally drained.

LEAST FAVORITE

An active dislike of orange may indicate a rather sober disposition and in particular we might suspect that this is a person who needs to demonstrate a dislike of frivolity. This choice could indicate a tendency to self-doubt or feelings of insecurity.

YELLOW

FAVORITE

The reactions to yellow are often strong and complicated. Most people view it as a warm, cheerful color which reminds us of sunlight. In color analysis it has come to be seen as indicative of strong intellectual qualities, and those who choose it are likely to be of high intelligence. Yet it has been shown to be a color favored by mentally retarded patients. Yellow lovers are said to need to be in control and are quite domineering. A yellow personality is said to have a pronounced flair for talking and needs to be the center of attention.

LEAST FAVORITE

Yellow haters are said to be narrow-minded, petty, frustrated individuals. They are, however, not uncommon. Yellow is a color which many people find all too easy to detest.

GREEN

FAVORITE

Being the color of most plants green is readily associated with nature, fertility, growth and renewal. It is the color of spring. Color analysts claim that green types are well-adjusted but conventional and, above all, they have a sense of the balance of things. They also maintain that a taste for green indicates such an enthusiastic appreciation of good living that it is associated with obesity. Green lovers have a need to live in peaceful harmony with their surroundings. They are neat at home, and are efficient and trustworthy employees.

LEAST FAVORITE

This represents excessive conventionality. What green fanciers see as balanced, natural and satisfying the anti-greens find stultifying. Anti-greens are said to be overly cautious in life, which results in isolation and loneliness and a deep reluctance to try anything new. Green is, of course, traditionally the color of envy.

BLUE

FAVORITE

This is thought to be the color of conservatism, reliability, achievement, and introspection. Blue fans are thought to be dependable, materially successful and predominantly middle-class. If red is associated with the left, then blue has a politically right-of-center aspect to it. You will find no blue fanciers among the ranks of the revolutionaries, nor are they particularly innovative people. Those who are politically blue do not exhibit their allegiance as readily as those who favor red. Being a "blue" is much more of an inner feeling and does not require public display. There is, it has to be said, a certain smugness about blue-lovers.

LEAST FAVORITE

What about a dislike of blue? It may indicate a dislike of the rather smug, middle-class atmosphere which surrounds the color. Blue-haters may also be put off by the cold, uncomfortable feeling blue gives them. It is not a jolly color and there are those who resent its rather introverted, thoughtful and sometimes sad associations.

PURPLE

FAVORITE

This is a rather showy color associated with a love of display. It is not coincidence that purple was the color favoured by Roman emperors. The mollusc shells which were used to produce the famous Tyrian purple dye were so highly prized that men would fight bitter wars over

them. Nowadays purple is often regarded as a bit over-the-top. Writing with purple ink on lavender notepaper, for example, would at one time be seen as a sign of a refined, sensitive nature, but today indicates an immature urge to impress. Someone with a pronounced taste for the color would either be one of life's more outrageous extroverts or, more probably, would be exhibiting very strong feelings of insecurity for which they felt the need of a psychological crutch.

LEAST FAVORITE

Hating purple is not hard. People who favor subtlety and eschew display will find this color hard to live with, particularly when it comes to clothing and personal adornment. Perhaps the garden is the one place where purple is still allowed to flourish unchecked. No one holds purple flowers responsible for their outlandish dress sense.

BROWN

FAVORITE

A bit boring, isn't it? Earthy, dull but very respectable, that is about the best you can say for brown-lovers. No color analyst will ever accuse them of being full of joie de vivre. This is the color of practical, down-to-earth people who disapprove of flightiness and excessive high spirits. In our grandparents' day you could have your front door painted any color you liked as long as it was brown! Nothing could be more respectable, or more boring. However, brown is the color of earth and also of the dung which fertilizes the earth. It has strong connections with growth and the survival of the natural order. But exciting it isn't. The most exciting thing you can think of about brown is that it's the color of chocolate.

LEAST FAVORITE

Not liking brown is one thing but hating it is quite another. It is such a sensible, serviceable color that to actually hate it seems like an unwarranted act of aggression. Brown-haters could feel a nagging doubt about how colorful their own personalities really are.

BLACK

FAVORITE

Black is really very interesting. Its association with death makes it largely unpopular but, humans are contrary creatures and, by some sort of reverse psychology, black has acquired an aura of danger and romance. There are many who find black a sign of sophistication and who consciously adopt the color for that reason. Of course, whole articles have been written about the psychological and social significance of that essential garment, the black leather jacket. Nothing could so readily embody the way in which black has been adopted by some as a totem. For them it signifies not death but revolt, excitement, style, and sex.

LEAST FAVORITE

There is nothing very unusual in hating black, it's mournful overtones make it a color which is easy to dislike. However, should the dislike be too pronounced it might be a sign of some powerful underlying anxiety.

WHITE

FAVORITE

White has come to symbolize cleanliness and purity but it lacks any emotional warmth. However, there is one area in which white is often deliberately chosen by people wishing to make a powerful statement and that is when choosing a car color. A white car has nothing to do with purity or hygiene - it is chosen specifically to demonstrate power and status.

LEAST FAVORITE

White is seldom anyone's first choice of color. It is cold, sterile, and lacking emotion. It is the color of virginity, purity, and squeaky-clean hygiene and, admirable though these qualities may be, if we are honest we do not normally put them very high on our list of priorities.

Summary of colors and the personality traits with which they are commonly associated:

RED:	BLUE:
Temperamental	Retiring
Outgoing	Accommodating
Assertive	Reserved
Enthusiastic	Sensitive
Tense-driven	Self-doubting

YELLOW:	PURPLE:
Direct	Detail conscious
Confident	Socially bold
Self-sufficient	Conceptual
Disciplined	Radical

GREEN:	ORANGE:
Flexible	Group-oriented
Factual/realistic	Informal
Conventional	Outgoing
Relaxed	Radical

BROWN:	BLACK:
Cautious	Negative
Trusting	Lacking control
Calm/Stable	
	WHITE:
Restrained	Practical

THE COLOR CHOICES

We decided to give a color preference test to a group of people who had already undergone a personality profile analysis to compare the two sets of results and see how often those with the same personality trait chose the same color.

The personality profile test we used was constructed using sample data from 5649 members of the general public. For the color preference test we decided to use only those candidates whose individual score in the personality profile test was in the top 20% of any given trait, e.g. we regarded someone as assertive if he or she scored higher in this trait than 80% of the overall sample. We called this top 20% the "Significant Score". Each candidate was shown swatches of a set of colors (red, orange, blue, green, yellow, purple, brown, black, and white) and asked to choose their favorite three colors in order of preference and then to nominate the color they disliked most. The results below compare the color preferences chosen by specific personality traits. How does your personal analysis conform with our survey?

COLOR CHOICES (FROM SAMPLE OF 100)

1ST CHOICE		2ND CHOICE		3RD CHOICE	
Red	39	Green	23	Purple	27
Blue	31	Red	19	Orange	25
Green	19	Blue	17	Yellow	23
Yellow	5	Purple	13	Green	17
Orange	3	Orange	13	Blue	8
Purple	3	Yellow	12		
Black	3				

PERSONALITY TRAITS AND COLOR CHOICES

Trait	No. with Sig. Score	Red	Blue	Green	Yellow	Orange	Purple
Tense-driven	35	24	4	1	3	2	1
Assertive	34	18	5	3	3	2	3
Trusting	25	5	13	5	2	0	3
Radical	19	13	0	0	1	2	3
Disciplined	18	6	5	3	4	0	0

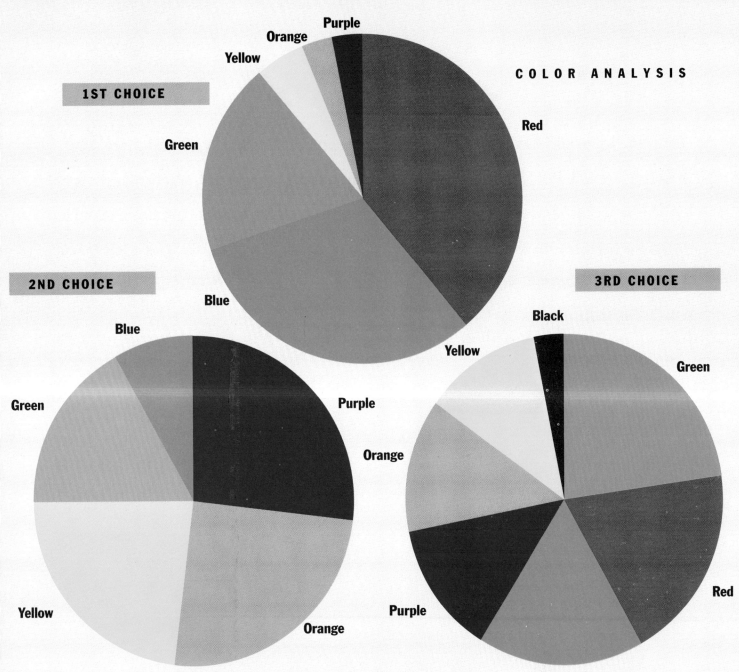

COLOR ANALYSIS

1ST CHOICE

2ND CHOICE

3RD CHOICE

% of 1st color choice with Significant Score for each trait

	Tense-driven	Assertive	Trusting	Radical	Disciplined
Red	62	46	13	33	15
Blue	13	16	42	0	16
Green	5	16	26	0	16
Yellow	60	60	40	20	80
Orange	67	67	0	67	0
Purple	33	100	0	100	0

The graph below shows the number of people from our sample with a Significant Score on each trait together with their 1st color choices. From the graph it appears that people who chose red as their first color dominate all the traits. This says much for the powerful attraction of red but rather confuses the issue of whether color is linked to personality. Of course, with a rather small sample of 100 people it is hard to get as much diversity as one would like. However, some interesting facts emerge.

Number of people with Significant Scores

| Tense-driven | Assertive | Trusting | Radical | Disciplined |

TRAIT

Twenty-four people chose red as their first color and had a Significant Score in the tense-driven factor of the personality test. This equals 69% of the 39 people who chose red as their favorite color, suggesting that there is a link between the choice of red and a tense, stressful personality. Assertiveness and a radical personality can also be seen as a dominating trait of red-lovers. On the other hand the trusting and disciplined traits are sparsely populated with lovers of red.

Although being tense-driven, assertive and disciplined were all approximately equal in distribution, the blue-lovers come across as highly trusting yet also extremely conventional. Due to the absence of any Significant Scores in the radical trait, this would seem to indicate that being trusting and radical do not go hand in hand.

RED LOVERS

BLUE LOVERS

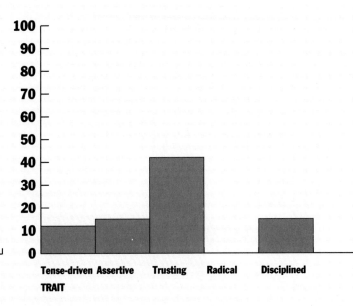

Love of green was not widespread among our candidates. They showed up largely in the trusting trait, made a small impact on the assertive and disciplined traits, and were almost invisible when it came to tension and stress.

The yellow, orange, and purple graphs all appear to be very positive with high percentages in several areas. The yellow-lovers come across as highly-disciplined, as well as being quite assertive and tense-driven, but they score very low on radical behaviour. Perhaps, alongside the red-lovers, the yellows score on every trait and suggest, overall, quite a balanced personality.

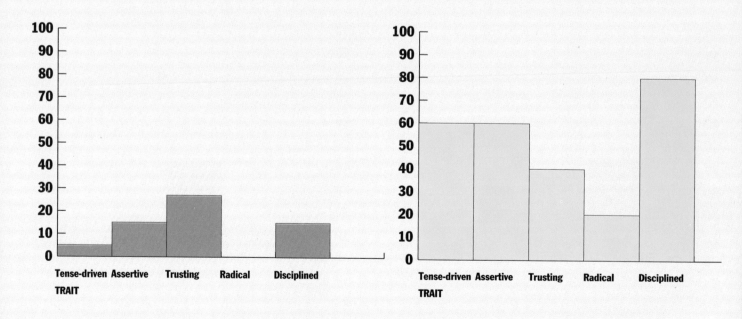

GREEN LOVERS

YELLOW LOVERS

Orange-lovers score highly on the tense-driven, assertive, and radical traits, supporting the previous suggestion that trusting and radical traits do not mix. It appears that orange-lovers are the opposite of the blues, being tense-driven, assertive, radical, but also suspicious and informal. Not a color to be worn if you want to be taken seriously!

Purple-lovers are strongly assertive and radical as they all scored significantly in those traits. This again supports the theory that being radical often goes with a lack of trust and discipline. The graph shows that purple-lovers have the most extreme characteristics with scores ranging from 0% to 100%.

ORANGE LOVERS

PURPLE LOVERS

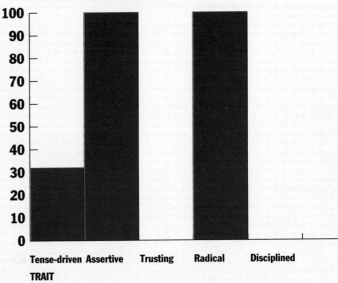

COLOR IN YOUR DAILY LIFE

It is one thing to analyze your choice of color from a selection of swatches and quite another to analyze the colors you have chosen to live with. The following test is designed to help you analyze your personal reaction to color in your everyday life, which in many instances may be governed by a whole range of subconscious elements. You are asked to choose colors in a variety of hypothetical situations. There are no right or wrong answers, and you can take as much time as you wish.

1   Look in your wardrobe. Is there one color which predominates? If so, what is it?   _____

2   Examine your business clothes. What colors do you choose for the office?   _____

3   Now look at your leisure wear. Do you have a favorite color?   _____

4   Imagine the outfit you would wear to a smart party. What color would it be?   _____

5   You are going on a date with someone you hope will be a new partner. What color would you wear?   _____

6   You are getting married (it's second time around and white is out) what color would you choose? (If you're a man you get to choose for your partner.)   _____

7   Think of the seasons of the year. Purely in terms of color, which do you prefer?   _____

8   You are going to buy a new car and can choose any color you like. What would it be?   _____

9   You are planning to re-paint the front door of your house. What color would you choose?   _____

10 Now re-decorate your living room. What color carpet would you choose?

_____

11 Re-decorate your bedroom. What color walls would you have?

_____

12 Choose new bed covers. What color would they be?

_____

13 When you re-decorate your home, do you tend to stick to the same color themes?

_____

14 Imagine a fine summer's day. Go into the garden and pick a bunch of flowers. What are your favorite colors?

_____

15 Imagine decorating a Christmas tree. Would you go for tinsel, baubles, and fairy lights or something more restrained and tasteful?

_____

16 You are a science fiction writer creating an alien world. What color would you choose for the sky?

_____

17 Do you find one color particularly calming? What is it?

_____

18 Think of a classic painting that has impressed you deeply. What are its main colors?

_____

19 Imagine yourself as a great artist and plan your next masterpiece. What color theme would you use?

_____

20 If you were forbidden to use one color ever again which would you be happiest to give up?

_____

21 A totalitarian government has passed a law forcing its citizens always to dress in the same color. Which would you choose?

_____

22 Some people imagine the days of the week as having colors. Try it. What are your choices?

_____

23 You are asked to launch a new political party. What color would you choose to represent it? (You may legally steal a color from any existing party.)

_____

24 You die and go to heaven. How do you imagine the color scheme?

_____

COMMENTARY

Most people stick to a very predictable color theme that they change only if they undergo some major change of lifestyle. The questions in this section are intended to get you to make color choices in as wide a variety of situations as possible. However, the probable result will be that you stick, for most purposes, to the same few favorite colors.

One way of assessing people's color choices is to liken them to the seasons. Thus there are people who prefer fresh spring colors (greens, yellows), bright summer colors (blues, bright reds, orange), or the more sober tones associated with autumn (brown, dark red, gold) and winter (grey, dark brown, black).

Look at your choices and see if you can detect a seasonal theme in them. Spring people see themselves as bright, enthusiastic, happy and spontaneous. Summer people have similar qualities but are more passionate and less ingenuous. There are more sophisticated versions of spring and summer coloring (using darker shades) for those who feel that age or social position will not let them express themselves as freely as they once did. People who choose autumnal themes go for an image of stability, responsibility, and maturity. Few people choose a winter theme, which indicates a very serious and sombre nature, though many are forced to hide behind wintry grey suits during their working day.

Now look at the color choices you made in the first test. How representative are your chosen colors in your everyday life? Sometimes a favorite color, such as red, might not be appropriate in an everyday environment, or are you trying to repress or hide a part of your nature by consciously not having that color around the house? If you are vaguely unhappy or dissatisfied with your surroundings, it could be because they don't contain enough of your favorite color which represents the essential you. See if some accessories in your chosen color will make you feel more content in your environment.

Look at the predominant color in your everyday life. If it is quite different from your chosen color, what does this mean? If you chose a very flamboyant color, but your everyday life is full of muted shades, perhaps you are a quiet, shy, thoughtful, and introspective person who wishes to be more outgoing. Alternatively, if your life is full of vivid reds and oranges but you chose the conservative blue as your favorite color, are you trying to pretend you are something you are not to those you encounter on a day-to-day basis?

EFFICIENCY

How efficient do you think you are? Are you one of those people who plans for all eventualities and never gets caught off guard? Or are you more of a "by the seat of your pants" type, who muddles through? This test will tell you the dreadful truth.

1 **Hungry friends arrive for an impromptu visit. Do you serve up:**
A) The stack of snack food reserved for such an occasion. ❑
B) Whip up a tasty meal in minutes. ❑
C) Phone for pizza - you've been meaning to go shopping for a while. ❑

2 **You are involved in a committee which is organizing a fund-raising event, but the planning is atrocious. Do you:**
A) Reorganize it completely for the better. ❑
B) Offer a few suggestions and let someone else put them into practice. ❑
C) You don't notice the bad planning. ❑

3 **When starting a new and challenging job, do you:**
A) Feel comfortable and familiar with everything within days. ❑
B) Continually ask other people questions about things which you keep forgetting. ❑
C) Feel able to ease into the job gradually, learning a little more each day. ❑

4 **You arrange to meet up with some friends for a night on the town. Do you:**
A) Arrive half an hour late - you couldn't decide what to wear. ❑
B) Wait for the others to arrive, having ordered the first round of drinks. ❑
C) Bump into your friends just as everyone arrives. ❑

5 **You have a hectic schedule at work. Do you:**
A) Get most of it done on time - you tried your best. ❑
B) End up doing it a week later as you didn't really feel very well at the time. ❑
C) Complete it and leave work early. ❑

6 **You attend a conference where you have various things to do and people to meet. Do you:**
A) End up talking to people, forgetting about the time, and being continually behind schedule. ❑
B) Frequently keep a check on the time, being where you should be without having to rush. ❑
C) Wait for someone else to tell you what to do, and then do it. ❑

7 **When you are due to catch a train to the airport, do you:**
A) Catch an earlier one to allow plenty of time. ❑
B) Miss it completely, and end up paying out some of your spending money for a taxi. ❑
C) Arrive at the station just in time, hoping that there will be no delays. ❑

8 Someone suggests throwing a surprise party for a friend and you get lumbered with the planning. Do you:

A) Phone everybody a few days before to arrange when everyone should arrive at your house. ❏

B) Issue invitations weeks in advance with precise details of what is happening. ❏

C) Accidently let slip to the birthday guest about the party, and end up going out for drinks instead. ❏

9 Your lamp stops working, and you suspect it has something to do with the plug. Do you:

A) Get out a book which explains how to check and rewire the plug, and follow the instructions carefully. ❏

B) Send the lamp to be repaired. ❏

C) Reach for the screwdriver, and rewire the plug within minutes. ❏

10 For a special occasion, you search for your best shirt which you last wore a week ago. Do you:

A) Retrieve it from the pile of clean washing, and give it a quick iron. ❏

B) Pick it up off the floor, dust it down, and put it on. ❏

C) Get it from the hanger, where it has been since you washed and ironed it three days ago. ❏

11 You recall the ambitions you had as a child - the job you wanted to do, the place you wanted to live. Do you:

A) Look around you, feeling pleased that you have, or are on the way to, fulfilling your aspirations. ❏

B) Decide to work a bit harder to achieve your ambitions in the future sometime. ❏

C) Laugh them off - you're quite happy as you are, without having to work harder just to fulfil a dream. ❏

12 After buying a new computer, you discover it is more complicated than you first realized. Do you:

A) Study the manual for a while, then dubiously start to use it. ❏

B) Take it back to the shop, and return with a simpler model. ❏

C) Switch it on, and persevere for a short while until you get the hang of it - it doesn't take long with practice. ❏

13 A child you know rushes up to you having scraped and cut her leg quite badly. Do you:

A) Faint. ❏

B) Comfort her while cleaning and bandaging the wound. ❏

C) Ask her if she can remember what normally happens when she has cut herself. ❏

14 Picture your home. If asked where to find a number of objects used infrequently, would you:

A) Calmly collect them all from their respective places within minutes. ❏

B) Give up, having created chaos looking. ❏

C) Wander around scratching your head until you finally collect most of the things together. ❏

15 You suspect that the house next door is being burgled and you think the owners are away. Do you:
A) Go back to sleep. ❏
B) Telephone the house in the hope of scaring the intruder off - if somebody answers, ❏
everything is obviously fine.
C) Contact the police immediately. ❏

16 When you wake up feeling not too great, do you:
A) Take a couple of painkillers, and venture out to face the world. ❏
B) Pull the blankets back over your head. ❏
C) Jump out of bed and keep busy - the more you do, the more likely you will ❏
forget about feeling ill.

17 You are driving along with a police car behind you. Do you:
A) Drive along in confidence - you saw it pull out behind you at the last junction, ❏
and have been cautious ever since.
B) Slam on the breaks as you are driving a bit too fast. ❏
C) Not notice that you are exceeding the limit until it starts flashing its lights and ❏
its siren goes on.

18 You are owed a reasonably large amount of money by a client. Do you:
A) Write it off as one of those things. ❏
B) Write a letter threatening legal action, and then wait for them to pay up. ❏
C) Take them to court - it may be complicated but it's no great hassle. ❏

19 You decide to buy a house, but you have never made such a move before. Do you:
A) Seek advice from as many sources as possible, and move in to the house you ❏
want without any avoidable trouble.
B) Find that it's too complicated, and carry on renting instead. ❏
C) Start out on a long and weary process, eventually moving into the third house ❏
which you wanted.

20 You have an important exam looming over you. Do you:
A) Open a few books in between going out and watching television. ❏
B) Plan a comprehensive revision schedule and stick to it. ❏
C) Forget about it until the night before, panic, and cram until the the early hours. ❏

21 After being set a project at work for which there is a deadline, do you:
A) Organize your time with care so you can hope to meet the deadline. ❏
B) Stay late for a week before, drink lots of coffee to stay awake, and somehow ❏
manage to hand it in on time.
C) Hand it in early, and start on the next project ahead of schedule. ❏

22 The office filing system leaves a lot to be desired. Do you:
A) Reorganize it completely, making it much more efficient. ❏
B) Improve individual sections, but neglect the overall problem. ❏
C) You always get someone else to use it for you. ❏

23 **You are due to start work at 9, but are late, what is your most likely reason for delay:**
A) You overslept. ❏
B) Your car broke down. ❏
C) A freak snowstorm - normally you're never late. ❏

24 **A new rule is introduced at work which causes much annoyance. Do you:**
A) Organize a petition opposing the rule. ❏
B) Learn to adjust to it. ❏
C) Grumble about it with colleagues. ❏

25 **You've got a headache, the television's on the blink and the kids are rioting. Do you:**
A) Scream until the children are terrorized into silence. ❏
B) Take some aspirin, arrange for the t.v. to be repaired while organizing a game which all the children can play and enjoy. ❏
C) Ask a friend to watch the children and lie down for a few minutes. ❏

26 **You've decided to clear out the attic for conversion into a spare bedroom. Do you:**
A) Set aside a few days to clear it out, sorting through things gradually, getting distracted by inspecting things you thought were lost forever. ❏
B) Rope some friends into helping you clean up, but end up partying instead. ❏
C) Blitz the attic, throwing out all the junk for the next refuse collection, feeling it's a job well done. ❏

27 **It's time to start thinking about a holiday. Do you:**
A) Plan a self-catering tour, booking in advance, knowing exactly where you will be throughout. ❏
B) Dash down to the travel agents at the last minute, booking a bargain to a place you've never really thought about before. ❏
C) Peruse the travel brochures until you find and book a trip to a place which you have always wanted to visit. ❏

28 **You arrange to meet a friend in a town a fair distance away whose roads you are completely unfamiliar with. Do you:**
A) Plan a route by train, and eventually meet your friend with the help of half a dozen people in the town giving you directions. ❏
B) Drive there, having studied the map carefully, and find your friend without any major problems. ❏
C) Tell your friend that you are really unsure about the route, and ask if you can meet somewhere closer to home. ❏

29 **You decide to have a small dinner party at home for a few close friends. Do you:**
A) Cook a delicious meal using the fresh ingredients you bought in the morning. ❏
B) Serve some pre-packaged meals with ready-made salad. ❏
C) Cook one of your few dishes which all your friends have had before, and joke about each time they come for dinner. ❏

HOW EMOTIONAL ARE YOU?

Do you burst into tears at the slightest provocation, or are you totally unmoved by anything small and fluffy? Do you take things to heart, or do you have a more pragmatic attitude to life? Answer the following questions and all will be revealed.

1   **You've just bought an expensive vase but when you get home you accidentally drop it and it breaks into many pieces. Do you:**
A) Curse your own stupidity while picking up the pieces to throw away. ❏
B) Look down in absolute horror, spending the afternoon crying your eyes out in ❏
total misery.
C) Look on it as one of those things, and start saving for a replacement. ❏

2   **You are laid off at work due to staff cuts. When you are told, do you:**
A) Angrily demand adequate compensation or else threaten to take the company to court ❏
for wrongful dismissal.
B) Start looking around for another job immediately. ❏
C) Irrationally declare all your grievances against the company, insulting the ❏
management so much that they threaten to call the police.

3   **Your much loved cat is run over and later dies after you've taken it to the vet. Do you:**
A) Lock yourself away in your distress, and emerge to face the world a day or two later. ❏
B) Cry uncontrollably and swear to seek revenge on the reckless driver. ❏
C) Put on a brave face, mourning in private. ❏

4   **You open a letter saying you have won the lottery, money which you have only ever dreamed of. Do you:**
A) Jump up and down, rushing out into the street in whatever your state of dress, yelling ❏
your news to the world.
B) Walk around in a daze, telling anyone who will listen. ❏
C) Call up your closest friends and relatives after you have got over the initial shock, telling ❏
them your news quite calmly.

5   **You're driving in the middle of nowhere when your car breaks down. You have little mechanical knowledge, so do you:**
A) Kick the car in a complete fury in the hope that this will miraculously bring it back to life. ❏
B) Lock up the car and start walking to the nearest house to call for help. ❏
C) Sit there in complete bewilderment, then wave furiously when you see another vehicle ❏
approach to get some help.

6   **After finding a note in your partner's jacket which suggests that she/he has been unfaithful to you, do you:**

A) Rationally ask for an explanation, then, if still dissatisfied, discuss the state of your relationship. ❑

B) Demand to know what is going on, initially seething with anger but then getting the situation into perspective. ❑

C) Explode at your partner, without giving him/her a chance to explain, culminating in a furious argument. ❑

7   **You get to work one morning but at lunchtime you discover that your gold pen is missing. Do you:**

A) Angrily declare that it must have been stolen and demand to search all of your colleagues' bags. ❑

B) Calmly ask if anyone has seen it and, if not, wait until you can get home to search properly. ❑

C) Remain unruffled and carry out a thorough search at work, but become more panicky when it doesn't appear. ❑

8   **You are helping a friend to prepare some dinner when he cuts himself badly, and blood starts gushing out of his arm. Do you:**

A) Look on in bewilderment but then swing into action, dashing over to get bandages and painkillers. ❑

B) Scream when you see all the blood, asking him what you should do while being incapable of doing anything. ❑

C) Clean and dress the wound as quickly as possible, managing to contain your own distress. ❑

9   **An aunt always sends you cards and presents for your birthday, but you suddenly discover you have forgotten that today is her birthday and you haven't done anything for her. Do you:**

A) Ring her up, apologizing profusely, begging forgiveness for your forgetfulness. ❑

B) Dash down to the nearest shop to get a card and a gift, posting them at once with an apology for being late. ❑

C) Wonder what to do, spending so long worrying about it that the shops shut before you are able to buy a card. ❑

10   **Police unexpectedly arrive at your door, arresting you on suspicion of a burglary you have not committed. Do you:**

A) Declare your innocence, refusing to go willingly with them to the station, lashing out at them during their attempts to come near. ❑

B) Ask them what on earth they are talking about and demand to talk to one of their superiors before going anywhere. ❑

C) Rationally declare your innocence, agreeing to come to the station to help with enquiries as soon as you have contacted your solicitor. ❑

11 You are delivered the wrong newspaper for the third day running. Do you:
A) Rush to the newsagents, demanding to know what is going on. ❒
B) Telephone the newsagents, informing them of their mistake, asking if they could ❒
kindly get it right in future.
C) Wait for the following morning's delivery to give the delivery boy a torrent of ❒
verbal abuse.

12 You are in the process of frying some potatoes when the pan suddenly catches fire. Do you:
A) Take the pan off the heat, and quickly cover it with a damp cloth to end the crisis. ❒
B) Run outside yelling "fire! fire!", being too panic-stricken to do anything. ❒
C) Start to panic, but manage to throw a cloth over the pan before removing it from ❒
the heat in-between your cursing.

13 You arrive home to discover that the water pipes have burst, and water is flooding into your
home. Do you:
A) Yell for help while madly attempting to clear the mess. ❒
B) Run to the nearest phone to call for help then return, carrying out the ❒
instructions you have been given before help arrives.
C) Look on in total panic before collapsing from the shock. ❒

14 You set off for a long walk on what appears to be a lovely sunny day, but suddenly a
torrential downpour breaks out and you are completely unprepared. Do you:
A) Carry on as before, treating it as part of the adventure. ❒
B) Run around dementedly, desperately searching for the nearest bit of cover. ❒
C) Curse the world, declaring it's just your luck, storming off in a foul temper in a ❒
search for shelter.

15 You return to a large parking area where you are now unable to find your car. Do you:
A) Try to stay calm, conducting another thorough search as you could easily have ❒
missed it.
B) Allow your panic to take control, yelling that it's been stolen, then calling the police ❒
in the midst of your hysteria.
C) Suspect the worst, dashing around the area looking for your car while you're wait- ❒
ing for the police to arrive.

16 You get your best white shirt out of the washing machine only to find that it has been dyed
pink. Do you:
A) Dig out some bleach and various other cleaning agents and set about whitening it. ❒
B) Ring up a friend in a panic, asking how on earth you can get the white back. ❒
C) Angrily kick the washing machine with your foot, stub your toe, and hobble ❒
around with a very pink shirt.

17 The service you receive at a restaurant is abysmal - you end up having to wait 40 minutes for the first course alone. Do you:

A) Storm out of the restaurant, making your dissatisfaction strongly known, and go and find somewhere else. ☐

B) Call the waitress over, demanding that your food is brought immediately or else you will leave. ☐

C) Ask for the manager, politely expressing your feelings until you get an apology and a substantial discount. ☐

18 You discover that your tape player has chewed up the cassette you have only just bought. Do you:

A) Painstakingly try to untangle the tape, but eventually give up and play something else instead. ☐

B) Contact the manufacturer at once, seething, complaining that the player is faulty and that you want compensation. ☐

C) Flare up in a temper, but quickly settle down in an attempt to fix the damage. ☐

19 Your friends have all commented that they cannot afford to buy much for your birthday, but when the day arrives, they present you with an expensive gift that you have always wanted. Do you:

A) Remain speechless with joy for a few minutes, then thank them properly. ☐

B) Examine the gift in great detail, eloquently expressing your sincere gratitude. ☐

C) Break down in floods of tears, unable to say anything properly so you hug everyone instead. ☐

20 You get home after an interview for a job you really want, convinced that you were successful. However, a few days later you receive a letter of rejection. Do you:

A) Shrug off the disappointment and look for something else instead. ☐

B) Fling yourself on your bed in abject misery, feeling a complete failure. ☐

C) Feel completely distraught until you manage to put things into perspective. ☐

21 After watching a film on television with a very sad and emotional ending, do you:

A) Reach for another box of tissues. ☐

B) Feel caught up in the moment, but then become involved in whatever follows it. ☐

C) Remain relatively unmoved as it was only a film, after all. ☐

22 You oversleep, eventually waking up realizing that you have 15 minutes to get ready to leave in time to meet someone. Do you:

A) Dash around in a panic, managing to turn up just a little late. ☐

B) Get ready as quickly but as calmly as possible - there are more important things in life to worry about. ☐

C) Spend so long getting in a fluster worrying about having overslept that you take twice as long as usual to get ready. ☐

23 You are sitting in your car at some traffic lights when someone drives into the back of you, making a large dent. Do you:
A) Start yelling at the other driver, getting the whole thing way out of proportion. ❑
B) Make sure the handbrake is on, then step out and start taking the details of the other driver for insurance purposes, ignoring the looks of the people waiting behind you. ❑
C) Sit there in amazement, wondering how anyone could let that happen, then wait for the other driver to approach before expressing these views to him/her. ❑

24 It's your birthday and you arrive home thinking everyone has forgotten but are greeted with a surprise party. Do you:
A) Immediately get into the swing, delighted that they haven't forgotten after all. ❑
B) Declare how upset you've been all day but secretly feel pleased. ❑
C) Stand there in astonished silence, coming close to tears, then express your delight. ❑

25 A woman suddenly arrives on your doorstep declaring herself to be your long-lost sister. Do you:
A) Cautiously ask for a few more details before inviting her into your home, feeling full of excitement. ❑
B) Throw your arms around her, unable to speak, waiting for several minutes before you start to question her. ❑
C) Feel sceptical until she reveals more about the situation, then offer to make coffee and have a chat. ❑

26 After returning from a trip abroad, you send your film to be developed, only to find that none of the pictures has come out. Do you:
A) Feel distressed beyond words, throwing the camera at the wall in your fury, despite the fact that it was your fault. ❑
B) Take the film and camera to a photographic shop, asking if there is anything they can do, and come away sure that you will not let it happen again. ❑
C) After the initial shock, complain bitterly, but write it off as one of those things. ❑

27 You embarrass yourself totally at a party when you get completely drunk, and the following day your friends take great pleasure in reminding you of your antics. Do you:
A) Laugh it off casually, making a mental note to do the same to them some time. ❑
B) Storm off in a sulk, annoyed with them, but even more with yourself. ❑
C) Accept the jibes for a while, but then declare how you don't think it's funny being taunted for three solid hours. ❑

28 Your boss seems to continually pick on you without reason and when you reach the stage that you cannot take any more she/he has yet another go at you in public. Do you:
A) Hand in your resignation there and then in a fit of fury, later regretting your over-hasty actions. ❑

B) Make a loud and pointed remark about his/her unfair treatment, threatening to take action if anything more is said. ❑

C) Stand there in silence, refusing to be drawn into an argument, but explode as soon as your boss leaves the room. ❑

29 **An aunt who you have not seen for years makes an unexpected visit. When you see her, do you:**

A) Exclaim what a surprise it is, inviting her in to greet her properly. ❑

B) Throw your arms around her in total delight, almost knocking her over in the process. ❑

C) Stand there in astonishment before being able to express your joy and welcome her in to catch up on lost time. ❑

30 **You get back from a trip to discover that your home has been broken in to, and many of your precious things have been stolen. Do you:**

A) Burst into tears, unable to do anything until a neighbour arrives to see what the noise is about and helps to calm you down. ❑

B) Pinch yourself to make sure you are not dreaming, eventually summoning the courage to look around and phone for the police. ❑

C) After the initial shock, make a list of what's missing ready to give to the police when they arrive. ❑

HOW INTUITIVE DO YOU FEEL?

Some people seem to have a knack of "knowing" things even before they have the full facts. They also claim to be able to make snap judgements about people, places and situations which, in due course, turn out to be accurate even though they were not based on any solid evidence. Other more prosaic souls regard this as mere fancy or attempt to offer rational explanations. The following test should show you the degree to which you are prepared to be guided by intuition.

1   **You go to a party where you don't know many other people. Do you:**
A) Go and introduce yourself to the people who you feel, from first glance, you would like to get to know better. ☐
B) Allow yourself to be introduced to anyone who wanders over - you don't make judgements on people until you've got to know them. ☐
C) Talk to anyone and everyone as you'll probably not see them again. ☐

2   **You wake up in the middle of the night having had a bad dream concerning the people close to you. Do you:**
A) Forget about it - it was only a dream. ☐
B) Find that some elements of the dream later become reality. ☐
C) Warn the people of your experience as your dreams often recur as similar episodes in real life. ☐

3   **A letter arrives from a friend who you haven't seen for ages. Do you:**
A) Feel glad as you've been meaning to send a letter for a while. ☐
B) Feel surprised - you had forgotten about him/her completely. ☐
C) Open the letter after having thought about this friend, and how you hadn't heard from him/her for some time. ☐

4   **You switch on the radio, and a well-known song comes on. Do you:**
A) Consider what a coincidence it is that you were singing it just before it came on. ☐
B) Try to remember the words as you haven't heard it for ages. ☐
C) Turn the radio off as you were playing the tune only last night and are a bit bored with it. ☐

5   **You decide to place a bet on a horse. Do you:**
A) Shut your eyes and pick out a horse at random, bringing your finger down on the list of racers - for once it wins. ☐

B) Put your money on the horse which you've got a good feeling for; your feelings normally find a winner. ❐

C) Ask a friend for a tip, but unfortunately the horse stumbles at the first fence. ❐

6 **When watching a quiz show, do you:**
A) Guess correctly who will win at the beginning. ❐
B) Watch for a while, then choose a likely winner based on their performances so far. ❐
C) Change your mind throughout the quiz about who you think will win. ❐

7 **You go looking for a new house. Do you choose on the basis of:**
A) The structure and state of the house. ❐
B) Whatever your partner/mother/salesman advises. ❐
C) Whichever one feels right when you enter. ❐

8 **When shopping for new shoes, you see a pair of trousers which catch your eye. Do you:**
A) Forget about the shoes and buy the trousers as you know you won't regret it. ❐
B) Walk past the trousers and spend a long time choosing some shoes which match your requirements. ❐
C) Buy the trousers the following week after further deliberation. ❐

9 **You're involved in a discussion with a close friend. Do you find that when they hesitate mid-sentence you:**
A) Suggest a possible ending only to have the friend say something totally different. ❐
B) Wait in suspense for them to finish what they're saying. ❐
C) Finish off their sentences, with their firm agreement concerning what you said. ❐

10 **You reminisce with your partner about the moment when you first met. Did you:**
A) Not even notice him/her until someone introduced you. ❐
B) Spot him/her across a crowded room, instantly going weak at the knees. ❐
C) Glance at him/her, feel pleased with what you saw, going over to let the relationship bloom. ❐

11 **You and a colleague at work do not get on at all. When you first met, did you:**
A) Dislike him/her the minute you met. ❐
B) Find that the colleague is not popular with the others, and decide to go along with them. ❐
C) Spend a while chatting before you discover that you do not wish to be friends. ❐

12 **The day before going on a long train journey you suddenly visualize yourself being involved in a serious crash. Do you:**
A) Cancel the train journey and go by coach instead. ❐
B) Try to forget about your visions and catch the train feeling rather anxious. ❐
C) Reject the idea as being caused simply by an over-active imagination, and catch the train as if nothing had happened. ❐

13 Some people walk past you in a shopping mall when you are sitting down. You form ideas about their jobs and lives in your head, and later discover that a friend who joins you knew the passers-by. After discussing your ruminations, do you find they are:
A) Fairly accurate, but the jobs you designated weren't too close to the truth. ☐
B) Uncannily similar to the extent that your friend suspects that you knew the ☐
people already.
C) So obscure that you spend ages laughing about your false impressions. ☐

14 You enter a raffle at a fair, having a strong feeling that you will win. Do you:
A) Return home empty-handed - you never have much luck. ☐
B) Forget about the raffle, lose your ticket, and go home before it has even been drawn. ☐
C) Proudly leave the fair with the fruit basket, one of the top prizes. ☐

15 You look after your parents' house while they are away, but they return early without warning. Are you:
A) Shocked, and have to rush around clearing everything up. ☐
B) You had a feeling they would come back early so you're already prepared. ☐
C) You kept the house in order just in case they came back at any time. ☐

16 When you take part in a board game which is based entirely on luck and good guesswork, do you:
A) Cheat. ☐
B) Win every time. ☐
C) Win and lose about as often as everyone else. ☐

17 You've been waiting for an important call from a colleague who said she would phone sometime over the next few days. Whenever the phone rings, do you:
A) Jump on it, expecting it to be the colleague every time. ☐
B) You've completely forgotten that the colleague said she would ring. ☐
C) Answer every call you get casually, until the phone rings at one particular time, and you ☐
know it is her.

18 A beggar approaches you and asks for money for a sandwich. Do you:
A) Give the money - you always feel guilty otherwise, regardless of whether it's a "real" ☐
beggar or not.
B) Decide whether to give money on the basis of whether you consider the beggar to be ☐
genuine or not.
C) Pretend you haven't heard anything as you've been swindled by people ☐
masquerading as beggars before.

19 When a little-known acquaintance asks you for a loan, do you:
A) Ask other mutual friends whether you can trust the aquaintance to pay you back, and ☐
make a decision based on that.
B) You never lend money as that way you'll never lose out from someone who doesn't pay ☐
you back.
C) Decide from your impressions of the acquaintance whether to lend them the money or ☐
not - you consider yourself a shrewd judge of character.

20 **When friends need advice about an important decision, do they:**
A) Ask you as your decisions generally come up trumps. ☐
B) Ask your opinions then, ignoring them, act on their own intuition. ☐
C) Ask if you can help find some information to help make an informed judgement. ☐

21 **You are asked if you want to go and play in a big poker game. Do you:**
A) Refuse - you lose so often that it's not worth it. ☐
B) Agree - as long as you limit yourself to a certain amount of gambling money, you'll be all right. ☐
C) Ask when it starts - you nearly always make an honest profit. ☐

22 **You and a friend decide to go out for a picnic but halfway through lunch it starts to rain. Having forgotten to watch a weather forecast, do you:**
A) Pull out the umbrellas you brought with you just in case. ☐
B) Do nothing - you are already sitting under a shelter as you had a feeling that it was going to rain. ☐
C) Get soaking wet. ☐

23 **During a family trip you suddenly come across a place you feel you already know despite not remembering any previous visit. Do you:**
A) Dismiss your feelings as being total fantasy. ☐
B) Wonder about your feelings, and whether you actually did visit the place as a child. ☐
C) Accept that you already know the place - you often have feelings of this sort. ☐

24 **You arrive home from work after having had the strong impression that something disastrous has happened. Do you:**
A) Telephone round your close relatives to make sure they are all okay, and find that one of them has become seriously ill. ☐
B) Forget about your feelings as soon as you have had them, and make yourself some dinner instead. ☐
C) Discover the following day that one of your friends has had an accident. ☐

25 **After arriving at an abandoned airfield you start to feel very strange. Do you later find that:**
A) You have the flu coming on. ☐
B) The airfield featured heavily in the Second World War, where many men were killed. ☐
C) A storm suddenly starts in the middle of an otherwise calm and sunny day. ☐

26 **You are given a surprise gift for your birthday. Before opening it do you:**
A) Have various ideas about what the present could be. ☐
B) Guess exactly what it could be, without having known before. ☐
C) Know what it is - you got someone to slip up and tell you last week. ☐

27 You're on a walking trip in the middle of nowhere and suddenly feel like you're being watched. You look around and find that:
A) A fellow walker is just behind you.
B) A flock of birds has just flown over.
C) You're approaching a river.

28 You start to feel strange for no apparent reason while out shopping in a store. Do you find that:
A) The air-conditioning has broken down.
B) You're coming down with an illness.
C) You've forgotten to feed the cat.

29 A major crisis is happening in Africa, news of which is just filtering through. Do you:
A) Find out more later when a friend fills you in on the details.
B) Already know as the radio has been on all day.
C) Suspect that something disastrous has happened while you are out, and rush back to see the news on the television.

30 When you're reading the newspaper you begin to feel that you are being talked about by someone nearby. When you walk into the adjoining room, do you find that:
A) Nobody is there.
B) Two relatives have been discussing your role in the household.
C) A friend is coming to the door to ask if you would have time for a chat.

WHO'S IN THE DRIVING SEAT?

This test measures what psychologists describe as the "locus of control". How far do you feel able to control what happens in your life? Do you believe that you possess freewill and make your own luck, or are you at the mercy of forces beyond your control? The following questions should help you decide. There are three possible answers to each question: Yes, No, Don't Know. Try to answer the questions as honestly as you can. There is no time limit but do not ponder each question too long, the "off the top of your head" answer will give the best results.

		YES	NO	DON'T KNOW
1	Most of life's major events are beyond our control.	☐	☐	☐
2	I always know where I am going in life.	☐	☐	☐
3	Our fate is mapped out from the moment we are born.	☐	☐	☐
4	Ultimately we have little control over how the country is run.	☐	☐	☐
5	I don't believe in destiny.	☐	☐	☐
6	You can't fight City Hall.	☐	☐	☐
7	Government removes our power to help ourselves.	☐	☐	☐
8	The strongest dictatorship can be overturned by determined resistance.	☐	☐	☐
9	We can achieve anything if we try hard enough.	☐	☐	☐
10	I sometimes feel I stand on the sidelines of life.	☐	☐	☐
11	I seldom admit defeat.	☐	☐	☐
12	Our power to help ourselves is strictly limited.	☐	☐	☐

		YES	NO	DON'T KNOW
13	I do not believe in free will.	☐	☐	☐
14	I sit firmly in the driving seat of my life.	☐	☐	☐
15	I sometimes feel that I drift through life with no real purpose.	☐	☐	☐
16	I view the future with confidence.	☐	☐	☐
17	I often feel helpless when faced with life's problems.	☐	☐	☐
18	There is no such thing as an insuperable problem.	☐	☐	☐
19	I do not need God to tell me how to run my life.	☐	☐	☐
20	I believe in my own ability to solve my problems.	☐	☐	☐
21	I believe we make our own luck.	☐	☐	☐
22	Our destiny is too powerful to change.	☐	☐	☐
23	I believe that I can usually triumph over adversity.	☐	☐	☐
24	We are all just pawns in a game.	☐	☐	☐

HOW LOYAL ARE YOU?

Loyalty is one of those old-fashioned virtues which affects every area of life – work, family and friends. It is something we expect from others, but how loyal are you? The following questions are designed to help you find out.

1   **You suspect that a close relative has taken part in a robbery. Do you:**
A) Confront her/him, and wait for the reaction. ☐
B) Telephone the police immediately with your suspicions. ☐
C) Say nothing in the hope that you were wrong. ☐

2   **You have been working for a small family firm for several years, where you have always been treated well and enjoyed your work. However, you are offered another job with a rival company that offers more pay. Do you:**
A) Reject the offer as you wouldn't want to upset your current employers. ☐
B) Ask your current employers for a pay increase. ☐
C) Hand in your notice. ☐

3   **You have been planning a trip with a group of friends for ages, but you have second thoughts when you meet a new partner who isn't going. Do you:**
A) Telephone your partner every day while you are away, casting a cloud over the trip with your pining. ☐
B) Cancel at the last minute as you are sure your friends would do the same to you. ☐
C) Promise your partner that you will send a postcard sometime, and have a wonderful time. ☐

4   **During the busy season at work, you become ill and are ordered to stay at home. Do you:**
A) Feel guilty, and rush back to work before you have recovered properly. ☐
B) Stay in bed as long as possible, taking a couple of extra days off for good measure. ☐
C) Recuperate until you just about feel ready to return to work. ☐

5   **A war breaks out in a nearby country, and you are called upon to carry out some sort of national service which threatens your personal safety despite being beneficial for the country. Do you:**
A) Find as many excuses as possible to avoid being called up. ☐
B) Pack your things, ready to begin service the following morning. ☐
C) Persuade the recruiters that you would be the most help in administration, away from the front lines. ☐

6 You always have a Christmas break, but this year you discover that a fire broke out on Christmas Eve, and your workplace is in desperate need of sorting out due to the damaged windows, danger to the public, etc. Do you:

A) Wait for your boss to telephone you before volunteering your services. ☐

B) Only agree to go if you are guaranteed to be paid double the usual overtime rate. ☐

C) Phone some colleagues when you hear the news, and arrive on the scene with coffee and Christmas cake. ☐

7 You are offered a substantial amount of money, equal to half a year's salary, to assist a rival firm with some industrial espionage. Do you:

A) Agree, asking if they will pay more for additional information. ☐

B) Refuse point blank, informing your boss of the rival firm's activities. ☐

C) Give in after months of pestering at a time when you are desperate for money. ☐

8 You share an office with your best friend, but a new worker arrives on the scene and attempts to break up your friendship by telling you that your "best friend" has been spreading gossip about you. Do you:

A) Ignore the new worker as you trust your friend implicitly. ☐

B) Casually ask some colleagues you have known for longer if they have heard anything going around, and act upon that. ☐

C) Accuse your former best friend of betrayal, refusing to have anything more to do with him/her. ☐

9 Your sister, who has just lost her job, asks if she can borrow some money to tide her over for a while, but you have little as it is. Do you:

A) Tell her you cannot afford it. ☐

B) Buy her a food parcel. ☐

C) Send her whatever you have, foregoing the jacket you were going to buy. ☐

10 You overhear your boss talking about dismissing some of your colleagues on unreasonable grounds. Do you:

A) Keep quiet as it's not really any of your business. ☐

B) Spread the word around your workplace of the boss's intentions. ☐

C) Discreetly ingratiate yourself with the boss to assure your own security. ☐

11 You return to work after finishing a shift only to find that an acquaintance has been consistently fiddling the books for her own personal benefit. She offers you the money to buy a car to keep quiet. Do you:

A) Spend the weekend looking around car showrooms. ☐

B) Inform your boss at once of your discovery. ☐

C) Refuse to be bribed, telling her that either she stops now or you take further action. ☐

12 **You take a well-earned break from a hectic period at work. During your vacation, do you:**
A) Spend the time wondering how the others are coping. ☐
B) Forget about work completely, returning home refreshed and relaxed. ☐
C) Leave feeling a bit guilty, but telling yourself how you've earned a break. ☐

13 **You decide to get a puppy to keep your older dog company. However, your dog takes offence, and becomes aggressive. Do you:**
A) Give the dog away as the puppy is much cuter. ☐
B) Separate the dogs as you don't want to get rid of either. ☐
C) Find another home for the puppy, after waiting a few weeks to see if the situation improves. ☐

14 **If you managed a football team, and were offered a large sum of money for your leading player, plus a little more for yourself, would you:**
A) Seriously consider the offer, eventually deciding that your team cannot afford to lose that player. ☐
B) Refuse - you owe it to your team. ☐
C) Try to get a higher payment before transferring your player. ☐

15 **You accidentally knock over your partner's diary, pick it up, and discover that she/he was involved in a fight resulting in a child being seriously injured. The police do not know that your partner is responsible. Do you:**
A) Make discreet enquiries about the child, and after finding that all is well, forget about it. ☐
B) Confront your partner about it, promptly informing the police. ☐
C) Mention it during dinner, and agree to act as an alibi if the need arises. ☐

16 **You have been banking with a particular bank for years, and know the staff, who have always treated you well and with consideration. You discover that the bank is losing clients to a rival company which is offering many incentives to join. Do you:**
A) Draw your money out at the earliest opportunity, taking advantage of the offers. ☐
B) Open another smaller account so you can benefit from both. ☐
C) Stay where you are until you cannot avoid transferring your money. ☐

17 **You are offered a large sum of money by a newspaper for a scoop concerning one of your relatives which could cause discomfort. Do you:**
A) Ask around, seeing if the other newspapers will pay more. ☐
B) Refuse, threatening court action if they print the story. ☐
C) Say nothing apart from directing them to another source for a small fee. ☐

18 **You are offered an even larger some of money by a newspaper for a story concerning the relationship of two of your friends who have confided in you. Do you:**
A) Threaten the newspaper with legal action if any story is printed. ☐
B) Say as little as possible, guardedly answering their questions in monosyllables, accepting some payment and demanding anonymity. ☐
C) Ask the newspaper if they will wait a little longer and pay a bit more for you to find out some more details. ☐

19 You accidentally overhear a juicy bit of gossip, but are then implored to keep quiet by the friends you hear talking. Do you:

A) Drop unsubtle hints to other people until everybody knows the gossip, then deny responsibility for letting the news get around. ❑

B) Phone a friend, telling him/her the news while asking him/her to keep it secret, suspecting that the news will be passed on anyway. ❑

C) Say nothing - you've forgotten the news already, and you don't like gossip. ❑

20 You have always voted for and strongly supported one political party, but find that all of a sudden this party has lost a lot of popularity. Do you:

A) Spend a while debating with yourself whether you should still support them - you don't want to become unpopular too. ❑

B) Campaign on their behalf - it will take more than this phase to deter you. ❑

C) Follow the wave of popular belief, discarding this party for another. ❑

21 You work for a small restaurant whose selling point is the warm friendly atmosphere. You discover you could make yourself some money by pocketing the cash paid for certain foods which are already cooked and which sit, uncounted, ready to be served. Do you:

A) Point this possibility out to your employer so the system is changed. ❑

B) Rake in the cash, feeling proud of your initiative. ❑

C) Carry on as normal, turning a blind eye to your fellow workers' underhand actions. ❑

22 The small company you have always worked for announces that it will have to cut wages in order to survive, but better times will come as a result. Do you:

A) Resign after finding another better paid job. ❑

B) Inform your employers that you will accept the pay cut, but not for long, and will leave if something better comes up. ❑

C) Volunteer to work longer hours as well to help the company get through this difficult time. ❑

23 You discover that your brother has been two-timing two girls, who you have seen once, but who are unaware of each other's existence. Do you:

A) Tell your brother how rotten you think it is and leave it at that. ❑

B) Inform your brother that unless he stops two-timing the girls, you will tell them what he is up to. ❑

C) Make sure that the girls know exactly what your brother is doing. ❑

24 You promise a friend that as soon as a job vacancy comes up at your workplace, you will put in a good word to help her/him get the job. However, you discover that someone who you find very attractive has already been interviewed and is being considered for a future vacancy. Do you:

A) Encourage your friend to come in and ask for the job but say nothing to aid his/her plight. ❑

B) Immediately inform the person who conducted the interview of your friend's skills and experience. ❑

C) Tell your friend that unfortunately there are no jobs available at present. ❑

25 A friend is counting on you to help out and act as a witness at her wedding, but a week beforehand, you are offered the chance you have been waiting for to work abroad for a week or two on condition that you leave within the next few days. Do you:

A) Plead with your boss to be allowed to go after the wedding, accepting your boss's decision either way. ❐

B) Explain the situation to your friend, making her feel so guilty that she implores you to go. ❐

C) Refuse the offer, saying nothing to your friend, and wait for the next opportunity to come up. ❐

26 You find out that your father, happily married until now, has been unfaithful to your mother. He begs you not to say anything and swears that he will end his promiscuous actions. Do you:

A) Inform your mother, regardless of the hurt and anxiety it will cause. ❐

B) Do as your father asks as it is not your business to interfere. ❐

C) Insist that your father discusses the situation with your mother, or threaten to tell her yourself. ❐

27 You go abroad on a trip with a pal, both of you being unattached, but you form a romantic relationship with someone when you are there, while your friend does not. Do you:

A) Neglect your friend, leaving him/her to do his/her own thing. ❐

B) Try to find someone for your friend so you can go out as a foursome. ❐

C) Spend the trip switching between the two, feeling forever in the middle. ❐

28 Your best friend goes away for six months, asks you not to forget her/him, and returns, finding that you have a new set of friends. Do you:

A) Explain that you have formed new friendships and things aren't the same anymore. ❐

B) Introduce him/her as your best friend and spend ages catching up on lost time. ❐

C) Let your former best friend come out with you, but make it clear gradually that you have other friends too now. ❐

29 Your partner is accused of sexual harassment, and you do not know whether she/he is guilty or not as the evidence goes both ways. Do you:

A) Give your partner all the support you can regardless of whether she/he is guilty or not. ❐

B) Ignore your partner's claims to the contrary, taking the accusations as the truth, and ruin your relationship. ❐

C) Discuss the matter with your partner as calmly as possible, feeling uncomfortable but believing what your partner declares is the truth. ❐

30 A once prosperous friend arrives at your doorstep having lost all his money and possessions through his own bad management. Do you:

A) Lend him a bit of money, directing him to the nearest shelter for the homeless after giving him a meal. ❐

B) Offer him food and shelter until he lands on his feet again. ❐

C) Tell him it's all his own fault, and let him get on with it. ❐

HOW WELL DO YOU HANDLE MONEY?

Some people have the knack of making their money go far even if they don't have much of it, while others with well-paid jobs always seem to be broke. Which are you? Do you shiver over one smouldering lump of coal while gloating about how much money you have in the bank, or splash out on a lavish lifestyle and hide from the bank manager? These questions should help you decide.

1 When you go out, do you:
A) Leave on all the lights. ☐
B) Turn most of them out. ☐
C) Switch on the light security system. ☐

2 You go out for drinks with some friends. Do you:
A) Buy the first round. ☐
B) Always manage to avoid buying the first drinks and then always be somewhere ☐
else when the next drinks are bought.
C) Just buy your own. ☐

3 When sale time comes around again, do you:
A) Buy lots of bargains, and nothing until the next sales. ☐
B) Buy a bargain if it catches your eye, feel pleased, but still be willing to buy ☐
something for its full price if you really like it.
C) Stay at home as it's not worth the bother, and you prefer to pay the full price for ☐
things in good condition you know you'll wear.

4 You go out to a restaurant, and order something exotic which you find you don't like. Do you:
A) Eat it anyway, so as not to waste it. ☐
B) Order something else as well which you know you will enjoy, putting the exotic ☐
dish down to experience.
C) Nibble a few mouthfuls, and fill up on rolls and dessert. ☐

5 You inherit a substantial amount of money. Do you:
A) Save a third, spend a third on yourself, and pay off some bills with what's left. ☐
B) Put it all in a high-interest account, feeling secure and content. ☐
C) Fly off on the trip of a lifetime, using what's left for spending money. ☐

6 After buying a pair of shoes, you find they rub uncomfortably. Do you:
A) Persist until you hardly think about the pain at all. ☐
B) Give them away to a charity shop. ☐
C) Wear them a bit, and then sell them at a cheaper price to a friend. ☐

7 When you receive your bank statement, do you:
A) Know exactly how much there will be in your account already. ☐
B) Not even bother to look at it as it's too boring. ☐
C) Feel a bit surprised at the balance, but be just about able to work out where your money went. ☐

8 You watch an appeal on television which evokes great sympathy. Do you:
A) Phone in with your credit card number, and give what they ask and a little bit more. ☐
B) Tell yourself you don't know what will happen to your money, and you don't really trust these charities anyway. ☐
C) After a few days send a donation you consider to be fairly generous. ☐

9 You reach for the tomato ketchup and find that the bottle is nearly empty. Do you:
A) Scrape around in it for a while, and then open a new one. ☐
B) Discard it immediately, and find a full one. ☐
C) Stand it upside-down so you can use all of what's left the next day. ☐

10 A huge telephone bill arrives when your bank balance is already suffering. Do you:
A) Wait until you next get paid, then send off a payment. ☐
B) Know that the bill would be big, so you saved a little extra each week to cover it. ☐
C) Leave it unopened - you might pay it after the next two demands. ☐

11 You see a stereo you really want, but you won't have the money for a few months. Do you:
A) Borrow the money from a better-off friend who owes you a big favour, and pay it back gradually. ☐
B) Go out and buy the stereo, ignore the bills, and eat beans on toast for the next month. ☐
C) Wait until your birthday, and ask your relatives for a contribution towards it, rather than buy it yourself. ☐

12 You have recently bought a new lawn mower, but then see another model at a knock-down price. Do you:
A) Buy it - when the first one breaks down, you'll have a spare. ☐
B) Ignore the offer - you already have one which, if well looked after and serviced, will last you a lifetime. ☐
C) Wonder how you are going to pay off the first one which you couldn't afford, let alone another. ☐

13 In winter, your home is very draughty and cold. Do you:
A) Throw on a few extra sweaters - a little breeze never hurt anyone. ☐
B) Put all the heaters on full power, not thinking about the electricity bill. ☐
C) Double-glaze and insulate the house little by little until both the draughts and the ☐
heating bills have subsided.

14 A friend faces financial and physical hardship when losing her job and, consequently, her home.
Do you:
A) Offer her a bed for a few nights so she can get work something out without ☐
having to worry about a base.
B) Give her as much financial support as you can until she finds another job - she'd do ☐
the same for you.
C) Consider it to be her problem - she should have handled her money better, like you, in ☐
the first place.

15 You spot some of your favourite cereal on special offer at the local store. Do you:
A) Buy only a couple of boxes as you don't want to get bored with it. ☐
B) Buy as much as you can afford - you'll be saving money in the long run. ☐
C) Choose another cereal - you've been eating the one on offer for the last few days. ☐

16 Your oven suddenly breaks down and has to be replaced. Do you:
A) Already have an emergency fund to cover such a situation. ☐
B) Manage to pay the deposit for a new one, and pay the rest in instalments. ☐
C) Eat takeaway pizza every day until the bank agrees to give you a loan to buy ☐
a new one.

17 You discover that a neighbour's child is in urgent need of money to pay for an
operation which can only take place in another country. Do you:
A) Hand over the money you were saving for your holiday, and take out an ☐
overdraft for your summer break instead.
B) Volunteer to arrange some fund-raising events, which could make more than you ☐
could give anyway.
C) Demand attention from the local newspapers, asking why the operation can't take ☐
place in this country.

18 You see something you really want in a department store, but which you haven't got the cash to
pay for. Do you:
A) Take out a credit account with the store, paying the high interest charges. ☐
B) Look around for a cheaper, second-hand version of the same thing. ☐
C) Decide it's not a necessity and will wait for a while anyway. ☐

19 **You decide to sort through your bills one Sunday morning. Do you:**
A) Spend several hours pouring over the red type, before giving up in despair. ☐
B) File away all the bills in folders kept for that purpose, and write the one cheque for ☐
the bill that arrived on Friday which you haven't yet paid.
C) Dedicate the day to getting on top of your finances, and working out how much of ☐
your income goes towards paying off your interest and other commitments.

20 **The tax man arrives to go through the papers for your small business. Do you:**
A) Prepare yourself for the worst, but feel reasonably secure that you can handle what- ☐
ever the tax man presents you with.
B) Flee the country in horror when you realize the debts you have accrued. ☐
C) Proudly present the tax man with your carefully arranged bookwork, confident in ☐
the knowledge that you have nothing to fear.

21 **You receive a tip for some shares you are convinced cannot fail. Do you:**
A) Forget about the bills and your conscience and buy some shares instead. ☐
B) Do some further investigation into the company and, only when you are certain, part ☐
with some well-earned cash.
C) Tell yourself that share values can fall as well as rise, and invest your money in a ☐
high-interest account instead.

22 **A colleague confides that she is deeply in debt due to a financial risk she took some years ago.**
Do you:
A) Nod your head in sympathy, having shared the experience last year. ☐
B) Tell her that money should be handled with caution and, though you feel sorry for ☐
her, be quietly smug.
C) Empathize with her, and hope that the small risks you have taken will continue to ☐
prove themselves worthwhile.

23 **You take on a part-time job to earn some extra cash. Do you:**
A) Save the extra money so you can comfortably afford the trip you want next year. ☐
B) Save a bit, spend a bit, and give the job up after a while after feeling too tired. ☐
C) Enjoy having the extra money to spend on the latest fashions and going out. ☐

24 **You reach into your pocket for some money to buy a newspaper. Do you:**
A) Search around for the change - you know it's in there somewhere. ☐
B) Bring out some change and hope that you have enough money left after buying the ☐
drinks last night.
C) Look in your wallet - you know exactly how much change you have in your pocket, ☐
and it isn't enough.

25   **A mail order catalogue arrives which advertises all sorts of things it claims you have always needed but never been able to buy. Do you:**
A) Order a few cheap things out of laziness. ☐
B) Throw it away - you can make do perfectly well without. ☐
C) Place a bulk order and wonder why the things haven't been available before. ☐

26   **Do you:**
A) Continually worry about money, and where it all goes. ☐
B) Relax in the knowledge that you can cope with anything Fate throws your way. ☐
C) Treat money as a mere necessity, and get on with the really important things in your life. ☐

27   **Do you let money:**
A) Dictate your activites and lifestyle completely. ☐
B) Play little part in deciding what you do - there are more important things to worry about. ☐
C) Rule your life to a certain extent, but never let it damage your state of mind. ☐

28   **You come home exhausted after a long day at work, seeking relaxation. Do you:**
A) Take a shower as it's cheaper than a bath. ☐
B) Take a shower as you prefer them. ☐
C) Have a bath - the benefits outweigh the cost by far. ☐

29   **You are shopping for a new home computer. Do you:**
A) Look for the best deal, even if you have to trek round all day. ☐
B) Buy the expensive computer you saw advertised on television. A friend said it is brilliant and it comes with a free programme. ☐
C) Look around the first shop thoroughly until you find something which suits your tastes and your pocket. ☐

30   **You're on vacation and take out your last traveller's cheque on the last day. Do you:**
A) Gamble it on a game in the hope of doubling your money. ☐
B) Spend the day walking around and spending very little - you want to have some money for the journey home. ☐
C) Carry on quite happily as you have before - there's no need to start being extravagant now. ☐

COMMENTARIES

ASSERTIVENESS

A score of 25 or over labels you as a tough customer who has no trouble in making your views known. However, people may find you rather overbearing. If you scored in the lower 20s, you still find no trouble in asserting yourself but you can also exercise tact when needed. If you scored 20 you tend to take the easy path wherever possible but on occasions, when you feel especially aroused, you are capable of taking a stand. A negative score indicates you are too much of a pushover.

SCORING

	A)	B)	C)		A)	B)	C)		A)	B)	C)
1.	-1	1	0	11.	0	1	-1	21.	-1	1	0
2.	1	0	-1	12.	-1	1	0	22.	1	0	-1
3.	0	1	-1	13.	0	-1	1	23.	-1	1	0
4.	-1	0	1	14.	0	1	-1	24.	-1	0	1
5.	0	1	-1	15.	-1	0	1	25.	0	-1	1
6.	0	-1	1	16.	0	1	-1	26.	1	-1	0
7.	-1	1	0	17.	1	0	-1	27.	1	0	-1
8.	-1	0	1	18.	0	-1	1	28.	0	-1	1
9.	0	-1	1	19.	-1	1	0	29.	1	-1	0
10.	1	0	-1	20.	1	0	-1	30.	0	-1	1

MORAL/PHYSICAL COURAGE

Scored the maximum of 30? Anything over 25 puts you in the Indiana Jones league and your life will be filled with honour, integrity and medical bills. The middle ground is, as usual, probably the safest bet. A score of 18-23 would make you brave enough to hold your head high while ensuring that it still stays firmly attached to your shoulders. If you have a negative score we'll know you by the white feather in your button hole and the broad yellow stripe down your back.

SCORING

	A)	B)	C)		A)	B)	C)		A)	B)	C)
1.	-1	1	0	11.	1	-1	0	21.	0	1	-1
2.	1	0	-1	12.	0	-1	1	22.	-1	1	0
3.	0	-1	1	13.	-1	1	0	23.	-1	1	0
4.	-1	1	0	14.	-1	1	0	24.	-1	1	1
5.	1	0	-1	15.	1	-1	0	25.	1	-1	0
6.	-1	1	0	16.	-1	1	0	26.	-1	0	1
7.	1	0	-1	17.	1	0	-1	27.	1	0	-1
8.	1	0	-1	18.	0	1	-1	28.	-1	1	0
9.	0	1	-1	19.	1	0	-1	29.	1	0	-1
10.	1	0	-1	20.	0	1	-1	30.	1	0	-1

DOING/THINKING

The maximum score for this test is 29. The higher you score, the more likely you are to be a person who prefers to act rather than think. Anything over 25 would suggest that maybe you should pause sometimes to consider the consequences of the things you do (and get some much needed rest!). Ideally, a score somewhere in the 12-23 range would give a nice balance between thought and action. If you scored below ten then you probably have beautiful thoughts, but are you ever going to do anything about them? If you have a negative score, dream on!

SCORING

	A)	B)	C)			A)	B)	C)			A)	B)	C)
1.	1	-1	0		11.	1	0	-1		21.	-1	1	0
2.	1	-1	0		12.	-1	1	0		22.	-1	0	1
3.	0	1	-1		13.	-1	1	0		23.	0	1	-1
4.	1	-1	0		14.	1	0	-1		24.	1	0	-1
5.	0	-1	1		15.	-1	1	0		25.	1	-1	0
6.	0	1	-1		16.	0	-1	1		26.	0	1	-1
7.	1	-1	0		17.	1	-1	0		27.	0	-1	1
8.	-1	0	1		18.	1	-1	0		28.	1	0	-1
9.	0	1	-1		19.	0	1	-1		29.	0	1	-1
10.	-1	1	0		20.	-1	0	1					

EFFICIENCY

The maximum score is 29 and if this is what you got you are super efficient. Anyone who scored in the 20s need have no real worries about their efficiency. They are cool, calm, collected and usually on top of the situation, but they also have a few heart-warming little failings. If you scored less than five, go back to bed, assuming you can find it.

SCORING

	A)	B)	C)			A)	B)	C)			A)	B)	C)
1.	0	1	-1		11.	1	0	-1		21.	0	-1	1
2.	1	0	-1		12.	0	-1	1		22.	1	0	-1
3.	1	-1	0		13.	-1	1	0		23.	-1	0	1
4.	-1	1	0		14.	1	-1	0		24.	1	-1	0
5.	0	-1	1		15.	-1	0	1		25.	-1	1	0
6.	-1	1	0		16.	0	-1	1		26.	0	-1	1
7.	1	-1	0		17.	1	0	-1		27.	1	-1	0
8.	0	1	-1		18.	-1	0	1		28.	0	1	-1
9.	0	-1	1		19.	1	-1	0		29.	1	-1	0
10.	0	-1	1		20.	0	1	-1					

HOW EMOTIONAL ARE YOU?

Score over 25 on this test and you probably have fewer emotions than a pet goldfish. If you scored below 10 then you are the sort of person who found *The Little House on the Prairie* a deeply moving experience.

SCORING

	A)	B)	C)			A)	B)	C)			A)	B)	C)
1.	0	1	-1		11.	0	1	-1		21.	-1	0	1
2.	1	0	-1		12.	1	-1	0		22.	0	1	0
3.	0	-1	1		13.	0	1	-1		23.	-1	1	0
4.	-1	0	1		14.	1	0	-1		24.	1	0	-1
5.	-1	1	0		15.	1	-1	0		25.	0	-1	1
6.	1	0	-1		16.	1	0	-1		26.	-1	1	0
7.	-1	1	0		17.	-1	0	1		27.	1	-1	0
8.	0	-1	1		18.	1	-1	0		28.	-1	1	0
9.	-1	1	0		19.	0	1	-1		29.	1	-1	0
10.	-1	0	1		20.	1	-1	0		30.	-1	0	1

HOW INTUITIVE DO YOU FEEL?

If you scored 25-30 your faith in your intuition is rock solid and no one will ever persuade you that you should consider a different method of reaching decisions. If you scored 20-30 you are quite intuitive but regard your ability as an adjunct to reason rather than a replacement for it. If you fall in the 0-10 category you are really rather unsure about making judgements based on intuition and, on the whole, distrust your inner promptings. If you scored below zero, forget it! To you, intuition is a closed book.

SCORING

	A)	B)	C)			A)	B)	C)			A)	B)	C)
1.	1	0	-1		11.	1	-1	0		21.	-1	0	1
2.	-1	0	1		12.	0	1	-1		22.	0	1	-1
3.	0	-1	1		13.	1	0	-1		23.	-1	0	1
4.	-1	1	0		14.	0	-1	1		24.	1	-1	0
5.	0	1	-1		15.	-1	1	0		25.	-1	1	0
6.	1	0	-1		16.	-1	1	0		26.	0	1	-1
7.	-1	0	1		17.	0	-1	1		27.	1	0	-1
8.	1	-1	0		18.	0	1	-1		28.	0	1	-1
9.	0	-1	1		19.	0	-1	1		29.	-1	1	0
10.	-1	1	0		20.	1	-1	0		30.	-1	1	0

WHO'S IN THE DRIVING SEAT?

Your locus of control is the place from which you percieve your life being run. If you have a positive score in this test you have what is known as an external locus and this means that you see your life as being controlled primarily by outside influences (fate, the government, God, other people). If your score is negative then your locus is internal and you feel very much in charge of your life and able to surmount your difficulties by your own efforts. Those with an external locus of control may well suffer from various degrees of pessimism, while an internal locus is indicative of an optimistic world view.

SCORE:
Give yourself 1 point for a Yes answer to questions 1, 3, 4, 6, 7, 10, 12, 13, 15, 17, 22, 24. A No answer to any of these questions scores -1. If you answered Yes to any of the other questions give yourself -1 for each; a No answer scores 1. The maximum positive score is 24.

HOW LOYAL ARE YOU?

As usual the maximum score is 30 and if you scored anywhere near that you are a loyal, decent human being. Even if you missed a few points and only got into the middle 20s you still have plenty to be proud of. Once below ten, your loyalty is getting doubtful and you are probably pretty much a fair-weather friend. Score below zero and your loyalty leaves a lot to be desired.

SCORING

	A)	B)	C)		A)	B)	C)		A)	B)	C)
1.	0	-1	1	11.	-1	1	0	21.	1	-1	0
2.	1	0	-1	12.	1	-1	0	22.	-1	0	1
3.	0	-1	1	13.	-1	0	1	23.	1	0	-1
4.	1	-1	0	14.	0	1	1	24.	0	1	-1
5.	-1	1	0	15.	0	-1	1	25.	0	-1	1
6.	0	-1	1	16.	-1	0	1	26.	-1	0	1
7.	-1	1	0	17.	-1	1	0	27.	-1	1	0
8.	1	0	-1	18.	1	0	-1	28.	-1	1	0
9.	-1	0	1	19.	-1	0	1	29.	1	-1	0
10.	0	1	-1	20.	0	1	-1	30.	0	1	-1

HOW WELL DO YOU HANDLE MONEY?

Scored over 25? Thank you for your time Ebenezer, now get back to your counting house. A high score in this test is for real tightwads. Even those scoring in the high teens and early 20s occasionally suffer from short arms and deep pockets. However, if you are a low scorer you might be more fun to have around but your accountant doesn't love you. Below zero indicates you have no idea of how to handle money and can never quite work out how it dribbles through your fingers.

SCORING

	A)	B)	C)			A)	B)	C)			A)	B)	C)
1.	-1	0	1		11.	0	-1	1		21.	-1	0	1
2.	-1	1	0		12.	0	1	-1		22.	-1	1	0
3.	1	0	-1		13.	1	-1	0		23.	1	0	-1
4.	1	-1	0		14.	0	-1	1		24.	0	-1	1
5.	0	1	-1		15.	0	1	-1		25.	0	1	-1
6.	1	-1	0		16.	1	0	-1		26.	-1	1	0
7.	1	-1	0		17.	-1	0	1		27.	1	-1	0
8.	-1	1	0		18.	-1	0	1		28.	1	0	-1
9.	0	-1	1		19.	-1	1	0		29.	1	-1	0
10.	0	1	-1		20.	0	-1	1		30.	-1	0	1